Informational Text in K–3 Classrooms

Helping Children Read and Write

Sharon Benge Kletzien
West Chester University of Pennsylvania
West Chester, Pennsylvania, USA

Mariam Jean Dreher
University of Maryland
College Park, Maryland, USA

INTERNATIONAL
Reading Association
800 Barksdale Road, PO Box 8139
Newark, DE 19714-8139, USA
www.reading.org

The International Reading Association attempts, through its publications, to provide a forum for a wide spectrum of opinions on reading. This policy permits divergent viewpoints without implying the endorsement of the Association.

Director of Publications Joan M. Irwin
Editorial Director, Books and Special Projects Matthew W. Baker
Managing Editor Shannon Benner
Permissions Editor Janet S. Parrack
Acquisitions and Communications Coordinator Corinne M. Mooney
Associate Editor, Books and Special Projects Sara J. Murphy
Assistant Editor Charlene M. Nichols
Administrative Assistant Michele Jester
Senior Editorial Assistant Tyanna L. Collins
Production Department Manager Iona Muscella
Supervisor, Electronic Publishing Anette Schütz
Senior Electronic Publishing Specialist Cheryl J. Strum
Electronic Publishing Specialist R. Lynn Harrison
Proofreader Elizabeth C. Hunt

Project Editor Janet S. Parrack

Cover Design Linda Steere

Web addresses in this book were correct as of the publication date but may have become inactive or otherwise modified since that time. If you notice a deactivated or changed Web address, please e-mail books@reading.org with the words "Website Update" in the subject line. In your message, specify the Web link, the book title, and the page number on which the link appears.

Library of Congress Cataloging-in-Publication Data
Kletzien, Sharon Benge.
Informational text in K–3 classrooms : helping children read and write /
Sharon Benge Kletzien, Mariam Jean Dreher.
p. cm.
Includes bibliographical references and index.
ISBN 0-87207-537-0 (alk. paper)
1. Language arts (Primary) 2. Exposition (Rhetoric)--Study and teaching (Primary) I. Dreher, Mariam Jean. II. Title.
LB1528.K57 2003
372.6--dc22

2003017361

For my mother, my sons Jonathan and Chris, and
my husband Damon—readers all!
SBK

For Peter and Silvia, both readers par excellence.
MJD

CONTENTS

ACKNOWLEDGMENTS

We gratefully acknowledge the teachers and students of the many primary classrooms we visited and worked in while writing this book. We have special appreciation for the following teachers and their classes: Helena Akeefe, Sandra Greim Connor, Sharon Craig, Michelle Koopman, Heather McGinn, Renee Miller, Kathy Simpson, Susan Smith, and Cathy Yost.

The research by Dreher and Baker referred to in chapter 2 was supported by a grant from the Spencer Foundation to Mariam Jean Dreher and Linda Baker. The data presented, the statements made, and the views expressed are the sole responsibility of the authors.

CHAPTER 1

Informational Text in the K–3 Classroom: Supporting Motivation and Achievement

Why do primary-grade teachers need a book about using informational text? Informational text, written with the purpose of informing or persuading an audience, is factual. For example, it includes reports, biographies, autobiographies, histories, essays, textbooks, reference books, and magazines and newspapers. Because young children's reading instruction has typically involved stories, many educators believe that a book on using informational text would be more appropriate for intermediate-grade, middle school, and secondary school teachers. Yet as we will explain in this chapter, increasing evidence shows that young children benefit when teachers include informational text in reading instruction and that knowledge acquisition through reading should be an integral part of learning to read from an early age. There are several reasons that this is true:

- Advances in technology and information put additional literacy demands on all readers.
- Most of what children read outside of reading class is informational, and most of what they will need to read as adults is informational text.
- Educational organizations and state and national standards call for even young children to be effective readers of information.
- Standardized tests measuring young children's literacy achievement include informational text.

- ◆ Children who read more than one type of text have higher reading achievement.
- ◆ Informational text has motivational potential.
- ◆ Children *like* informational text.
- ◆ For some children, informational text provides a way into literacy that stories cannot.

In this chapter, we will elaborate on these reasons and explain why it is crucial for teachers to use informational text with children in K–3 classrooms. In doing so, we will draw on research and our own extensive experience, which includes a combined 27 years teaching preschool through 12th grade. As teacher educators and researchers, we have an additional 33 years working alongside teachers and children in classrooms exploring the use of informational text. We also have supervised university reading centers in which teachers and children have been actively engaged with both informational text and stories. Our experiences have led us to value the educational possibilities of informational text for teaching reading as well as for extending content area knowledge.

We are not suggesting, however, that teachers add to an already full curriculum or that they discontinue using stories with young children. Rather, we propose that they examine their reading selections and replace some stories with informational text. Much reading instruction, including word recognition, vocabulary, and comprehension, can be accomplished through informational text as well as through stories. A balanced mix of informational text and stories would provide a good introduction to the variety of genres that children are expected to read and enjoy.

It should be noted that although the term *informational text* seems clear, there are different types of informational text. In chapter 2, we describe in detail the various kinds of informational text written for young children. In addition, readers should note that we use the term *informational text* as some authors use *nonfiction*; this means that some sources that are quoted refer to *nonfiction* while others use *informational text*.

Stories and Informational Text in the K–3 Classroom

Most of the reading instruction done in the primary grades uses stories in spite of the fact that for more than a decade researchers have been pointing out the importance of using informational text (Hiebert & Fisher, 1990; Pappas, 1991). Ample evidence exists that most of what teachers use to teach reading and writing in the early grades is in story form. If teachers use a basal series, they find that informational selections provide approximately 16% of the content for second grade, according to a study by Moss and Newton (1998). In a survey, one group of primary teachers reported that they spend approximately 6% of their time reading informational text (Pressley, Rankin, & Yokoi, 1996). In a study of first-grade classrooms, Duke (2000) discovered that teachers spend approximately 3.6 minutes a day using informational text and that most classroom libraries do not include many of these titles. Popular read-alouds in primary grades do not generally include informational books (Hoffman, Roser, & Battle, 1993). Indeed, Venezky (2000) summarized the situation when he reported that literacy instruction in schools involves a steady diet of fiction and literary interpretation.

Expectations About Children's Reading and Writing

Even though most literacy instruction involves stories, expectations for children to be able to read, write, and learn from informational text are increasing as society has more access to a greater amount of information. To be able to find, understand, evaluate, and synthesize information across a variety of sources requires more sophisticated reading and writing strategies for informational text than has been required in the past (Kamil & Lane, 1997; Kletzien & DeRenzi, 2001; Leu, 2000). In order to develop these strategies, it is crucial that we provide children experience with informational text early in their developing literacy.

Today's K–3 children are expected to develop facility with informational text. The Committee on the Prevention of Reading Difficulties in Young Children reports that a successful learner in kindergarten "demonstrates familiarity with a variety of text genres including expository texts as well as stories and poems" (Snow, Burns, &

Griffin, 1998, p. 80). The committee further indicates that a successful learner in first, second, and third grades "reads and comprehends both fiction and nonfiction that is appropriately designed for grade level" (pp. 81–83). Additionally, the committee suggests that a successful second grader "interprets information from diagrams, charts, and graphs; reads nonfiction materials for answers to specific questions or for specific purposes; connects and compares information across nonfiction selections; [and] given organizational help, writes informative well-structured reports" (p. 82). According to the committee, third-grade students should be even more accomplished readers and writers of informational text. A successful third-grader

> summarizes major points from fiction and nonfiction texts; asks how, why, and what-if questions in interpreting nonfiction texts; in interpreting nonfiction, distinguishes cause and effect, fact and opinion, main idea and supporting details; [and] combines information from multiple sources in writing reports. (p. 83)

The International Reading Association (IRA) and the National Association for the Education of Young Children (NAEYC) in their joint position statement about developmentally appropriate practices for young children state that kindergarten children should "enjoy being read to and themselves retell simple narrative stories or informational text" (1998, p. 200). By the time children are in the third grade, they should be able to "recognize and discuss elements of different text structures" (p. 201).

Standards in many U.S. states also indicate that children should be comfortable with informational text by the time they are in third grade. For example, the Pennsylvania state standards (Pennsylvania Department of Education, 2003) require that children in third grade be able to "identify the purposes and types of text (e.g., literature, information) before reading" and that they "preview the text formats (e.g., title, headings, chapters and table of contents)" (p. 2). These standards also indicate that third graders should be able to "demonstrate after reading understanding and interpretation of both fiction and nonfiction text" (p. 3) and that they "read and understand essential content of informational texts and documents in all academic areas" (p. 4). The Virginia state standards require that first graders be able to read a variety of fiction and nonfiction texts (Virginia

Department of Education, 2003). Passages on the Wisconsin state comprehension test for third grade are one third nonfiction (Wisconsin Department of Public Instruction, 2003). These are only a few examples of what appears to be a widespread phenomenon—state standards that require young children to be competent users of informational text.

Not only do state standards require children to be able to read informational text, but this emphasis is also reflected in standardized testing used in the United States. Estimates indicate that 50 to 85% of the reading passages in standardized tests are informational text (Calkins, Montgomery, Santman, & Falk, 1998).

The United States is not alone in stressing the importance of young children's learning to understand informational text. Informational text is an important part of literacy instruction in England (Littlefair, 1991; Mallett, 1999; Wray & Lewis, 1998) and of Ireland's primary curriculum (Shiel, 2001/2002). In Canada, British Columbia reading standards also require that young children become proficient with nonfiction (British Columbia Performance Standards, 2003). These are examples of the apparent worldwide awareness of the importance of informational text for young children.

Improving Reading Achievement Using Informational Text

Providing a balance of genres for children to read helps improve their reading ability. Children who read a variety of materials become more accomplished readers (Dreher, 2003). The National Assessment of Educational Progress (NAEP) has documented that children who read a variety of genres generally have higher reading achievement than those who read only stories. NAEP results from 1992 showed that fourth-grade children who reported reading stories, magazines, and informational books had higher reading achievement than those who read only one or two types of material (Campbell, Kapinus, & Beatty, 1995).

Children who have had experience with informational text in the earlier years will be better able to read and understand these texts as they progress through school. Indeed, there are specific reading skills and strategies that are appropriate for informational text (and not for stories) that need to be taught. Rather than waiting until the intermediate grades to expect children to be able to read informational text and learn from it, we need to introduce these skills and strategies while they are learning to read.

Beginning Reading Instruction and the Information Reader

Some children, who might be referred to as "information readers," have difficulty learning to read using stories. For these children, informational texts can form the basis for teaching them to read and make the difference between success and failure in learning to read.

Information readers find information much more compelling than stories. Hynes (2000) describes a student who thought of himself as a nonreader because he liked to read for facts rather than for stories. As reading and writing facts became an accepted part of the classroom instruction, the student's attitude changed and his self-concept as a reader and writer grew.

Similarly, Caswell and Duke (1998) describe two children who struggled with reading and writing until their teachers recognized that they were much more successful with informational text than with stories. Once the children began working with informational text, they were able to progress much more quickly.

We also have seen children with whom we have worked come alive with interest when given the opportunity to read and write informational text. For these children, stories are not as compelling. The chance to read and write about a topic of great interest gives them the motivation to develop literacy skills. This has been true even for children who have been identified as struggling readers and writers.

Informational text has motivating potential because children are curious about their world. Curiosity is a powerful motivator for reading (Baker & Wigfield, 1999), and children who are interested in a particular topic are motivated to read about it in informational text. Alexander (1997) makes another point in explaining why informational text can be motivational. She claims that knowledge seeking contributes to readers' sense of self and also gives them an opportunity to learn about the world around them. They can become "experts" in areas of interest, giving them confidence in their ability to read as well as in their ability to learn and share their knowledge. For example, our experience working with Jimmy, a struggling reader, showed that when given the chance to read and write about trucks, his interest and motivation soared. He read and studied the pictures in several books and created a pamphlet describing his future plans for his truck sales and leasing company (see Figure 1). When he presented this to the other children in his class, his excitement

FIGURE 1

Student Informational Brochure

BRIEF INFORMATION

This brochure will help you discover information about our trucks.

- *Cab*
- *Frame*
- *Body*
- *Engines*
- *Styles*
- *Weight Capacity*

This is one of our gasoline tankers.

J. & S.
TRUCKING

J. & S.
TRUCKING
GO FAST
GO HARD

COME BUY
A NEW
2001
TRUCK
TODAY!

J. & S.
TRUCKING

ENGINES

We offer several different engines in all of our trucks. Our small trucks have V6 or V8 gasoline engines with automatic transmission. Our medium trucks have gasoline or diesel V8 engine with automatic or standard transmissions. Our large trucks have V8 diesel engines with standard transmission. All of these trucks will help with any of your needs.

This tanker carries liquids to the refinery.

CAB, BODY AND FRAMES

Our company makes good quality trucks. The trucks that we sell are panel trucks, platform trucks, cattle trucks, bulkhead trucks, automobile transport trucks, tankers and tractor trailers. All of our trucks come with options like:

- Bed
- TV/VCR
- Vinyl or Leather
- Power windows/locks
- Power seats with heat
- Air conditioning
- Heater
- GPS system
- Refrigerator
- Radio/Tape/CD

The frame and body are made of steel that will not rust. The frame, body and cab are the best in the country.

WEIGHT CAPACITY

We sell three types of trucks: heavy, medium and ligh Heavy trucks can carry cargo u to 15,000 to 20,000 pounds. Medium trucks have a weight capacity of 10,000 up to 20,00C pounds. Light truck's capacity load is 1,000 up to 10,000 pounds. Buy your truck for your weight requirements toda

and sense of accomplishment were evident. As the other students asked questions, Jimmy's confidence in himself and in his ability to read and write was strengthened.

Sometimes children who are struggling with reading and writing find informational text more appealing because the content seems more mature. Second or third graders reading on a primer level may be more comfortable reading an informational book than reading a story book at that level. There are many accurate, colorful informational books written at lower levels that may appeal to these young readers.

Reading Preferences and Informational Text

In classroom visits and informal discussions, we have heard teachers comment that children do not like informational books and say that they are boring and are too hard to read. Teachers are concerned that informational books are "anti-fun" (Warren & Fitzgerald, 1997, p. 356). In fact, there is evidence that young children are just as likely to choose informational books as they are storybooks (Kletzien & DeRenzi, 2001; Kletzien & Szabo, 1998). Pappas has conducted several studies that show that children enjoy and learn from informational books (Pappas, 1993; Pappas & Barry, 1997). In a recent study of children's reading preferences in England, Coles and Hall (2002) found that outside of school, both boys and girls read books, but they also read magazines and newspapers, most of which are informational. Therefore, children do like informational text, often choosing it over stories. As Dreher (2003) points out, a powerful way for teachers to motivate children to read is to provide them with diverse materials, making informational books an important part of balanced reading.

Summary

Primary-grade literacy instruction should include the use of informational text for both reading and writing. State standards, standardized tests, and national educational organizations recognize the importance of young children being able to read and understand information. In addition, children enjoy informational books, often finding them more motivating than storybooks. For some children, informational text provides an entry into literacy that stories do not.

The emphasis on using stories for instruction persists, however, in spite of the many voices that have been raised urging teachers to use more informational text in their classrooms. One reason that teachers may be reluctant to use more informational text is that they are less confident in their ability to design appropriate lessons. In the remaining chapters of this book, we suggest ways that teachers can develop their classroom libraries, choose quality informational text, and incorporate informational text into their literacy and content area instruction.

Throughout this book, we give suggestions for using informational text with all children in the primary grades. The suggested teaching and learning techniques work with struggling readers and writers, as well as with average or advanced readers and writers. Examples throughout are drawn from diverse classrooms that include children who read above and below grade level, children who have learning disabilities, and children who are gifted in literacy. Examples reflect urban and suburban districts and inclusion classrooms, as well as self-contained special education classrooms.

CHAPTER

2

Including Informational Text in the Classroom Library

In a position statement, *Providing Books and Other Print Materials for Classroom and School Libraries*, the International Reading Association (IRA; 1999) calls for "an immediate increase in funding for books in classroom, school, and town libraries" (n.p.). In taking this position, IRA states that libraries are important because "children who have access to books are more likely to read for enjoyment, and thus increase their reading skills and their desire to read to learn." IRA's position is rooted in research that documents the impact of good libraries on children's achievement. Indeed, both international evaluations and national assessments have shown that well-stocked classroom, school, and public libraries contribute to reading achievement (Elley, 1992; Krashen, 1995).

In this chapter, we focus on the classroom library because it is the most easily accessible library for most children and, hence, has the power to make a tremendous impact. Having books readily available appears to increase children's likelihood of reading them (Neuman, 1999; Worthy, Moorman, & Turner, 1999), and frequent reading is a strong predictor of reading achievement (Anderson, Wilson, & Fielding, 1988; Taylor, Frye, & Maruyama, 1990).

Although the classroom library is important for all children, it is particularly important for children who are at risk for developing reading difficulties. Many of these children come from low-income homes where few books are available to them (Smith, Constantino, & Krashen, 1997). Also, the public and school libraries in low-income neighborhoods are not well stocked in comparison to those in middle and upper middle class neighborhoods (Neuman & Celano, 2001; Smith, Constantino, & Krashen, 1997). This means that the classroom library may well be the main source of reading material for many children.

Yet children are often in classrooms with no libraries or with small collections that are not adequate enough to make a difference. In a study at the elementary level, Fractor, Woodruff, Martinez, and Teale (1993) found that 72% of kindergarten classrooms had libraries, but the rates for classroom libraries fell dramatically as children moved through the grades. The figures for first, second, and third grades were 55%, 52%, and 38%, respectively. Unfortunately, even when primary-grade classrooms had a library, over 90% were rated as basic, with a very small number of books.

Another difficulty with classroom libraries is that, whether large or small, they tend to contain mostly stories at the expense of informational books. Studies that have inventoried first-, second-, and third-grade classroom libraries indicate that they consist mainly of fiction (Dreher & Baker, 2003; Dreher & Dromsky, 2000; Duke, 2000). Yet children benefit from an opportunity to read and receive instruction about both fiction and informational text (Dreher, 2000).

The immediate access afforded by classroom libraries is crucial in helping children become skilled and motivated readers. But as stated, many classrooms do not have libraries, and those that do often have basic collections that are overwhelmingly fiction. What can teachers do about this situation? Teachers who do not have a classroom library need to start one, and those who do have a library can most likely improve it. The recommendations in this chapter will help in either case.

A well-designed classroom library needs to have an adequate amount of books and other materials. In this chapter, we first focus on books, discussing the types, numbers, and levels of books that are needed. Second, we discuss other resources (magazines, newspapers, and the Internet) that enhance children's opportunity to experience diverse types of reading. Finally, we discuss the design of classroom libraries and offer tips for obtaining resources and managing the library. In chapter 3, we expand our discussion by showing how to select books and other materials with an emphasis on quality.

A 50/50 Balance of Fiction and Informational Text

There is wide agreement that children need to be exposed to diverse literary genres. The Committee on the Prevention of Reading

Difficulties in Young Children (Snow, Burns, & Griffin, 1998), for example, concludes that primary-grade children must have the opportunity to interact with both fiction and informational text. Similarly, IRA's position is that "genres should include picture storybooks, novels, biography, fiction and nonfiction material, magazines, poetry, and a multitude of other types to suit the interests and range of reading abilities of all children" (IRA, 1999, n.p.).

Despite these calls for diverse reading materials, however, it is fiction that is evident in most classrooms. Thus, a prime concern for teachers is to change this situation, and the classroom library is an important place to start. We suggest that teachers aim for classroom libraries with an equal number of fiction and informational books. We base this suggestion on the argument that if children are to become equally proficient with both fiction and informational text, they need balanced opportunity to experience both types of text (Dreher, 2000).

Aiming for an equal balance of fiction and informational text is more complicated than it seems, largely because both fiction and informational text subsume many different genres. Fiction can include folk tales, fables, myths, fantasy, modern fiction, and historical fiction, and good libraries should offer children the chance to read all these genres. Similarly, if children are to fully experience informational text, class libraries should provide children with a wide range of informational text. Consequently, we next discuss important distinctions to be considered when selecting informational text for the class library.

Informational Text Can Be Narrative, Expository, or Mixed

Informational text (or nonfiction) sometimes has been equated incorrectly with nonnarrative or expository writing. For example, the following statement appeared in a recent book: "Until quite recently, the study of literature was divided into two major types of text structures: nonfiction (expository) and fiction (narrative)" (Buss & Karnowski, 2000, p. 3). But nonfiction (informational text) can be narrative, expository, or a combination of the two. To be sure that classroom libraries include a full range of informational text, we suggest that teachers distinguish among the three types: narrative-informational text, expository-informational text, and mixed text.

Narrative-Informational Text

Much informational text for young children is in a story or narrative format. The purpose of authors who write narrative-informational text is to convey factual information, but they use a story format because they believe this will make the information more appealing or easy to approach. These kinds of books contain story elements that include characters, goals, and resolutions. For example, *The Emperor's Egg* (Jenkins, 1999) provides much information about the life of emperor penguins as it tells the story of a male penguin who hatches the egg his mate lays.

> [W]hat's that shape over there? It can't be. Yes! It's a penguin! It's not just any old penguin either. It's a male Emperor penguin (the biggest penguin in the world), and he's doing a Very Important Job. He's taking care of his egg. He didn't lay it himself, of course. His mate did that weeks ago. But very soon afterward she turned around and waddled off to sea. (pp. 7–10)

Similarly, *Charlie Needs a Cloak* (dePaola, 1973) follows a shepherd through the steps of making his own cloak: "He really needed a new cloak. So, in the spring, Charlie sheared his sheep. He washed the wool, and carded the wool to straighten it out. Then Charlie spun the wool into yarn" (n.p.).

Many biographies and autobiographies for young children also are written in narrative form. *Snowflake Bentley* (Martin, 1998) won a Caldecott Medal for the story of a man whose fascination with snow led to the discovery of the uniqueness of individual snowflakes.

> In the days when farmers worked with ox and sled and cut the dark with lantern light, there lived a boy who loved snow more than anything else in the world.
>
> Willie Bentley's happiest days were snowstorm days. He watched snowflakes fall on his mittens, on dried grass of Vermont farm fields, on the dark metal handle of the barn door. He said snow was as beautiful as butterflies, or apple blossoms. (n.p.)

Expository-Informational Text

Expository-informational books do not include story elements such as characters, goals, and resolutions. Instead, these books might be characterized as reports, using expository text structures such as cause-effect, comparison-contrast, sequence, description, and problem-solution. Expository-informational books explain the natural and social world, including animals, places, and cultural groups. Examples include books from the Eyewitness Juniors series such as *Amazing Snakes* (Parsons, 1990), the Let's-Read-and-Find-Out Science series such as *The Skeleton Inside You* (Balestrino, 1989), the Pull Ahead series such as *Soaring Bald Eagles* (Martin-James, 2001), and the Picture the Past series such as *Life in America's First Cities* (Isaacs, 2000).

The writing in expository-informational books differs considerably from narrative-informational books, as the following excerpt from *Jungle Animals* (Royston, 1991) illustrates:

> This tiny green tree frog is so small that it could sit on your thumb. It hides from its enemies among the green leaves. Tree frogs have sticky fingers and toes. They cling to leaves and twigs, looking out for insects to eat. (p. 10)

In the excerpt, tree frogs in general are being discussed, rather than an individual frog as would be done in a story. Note also the use of present verb tense (timeless verb) to convey the sense that the characteristics being discussed apply in general, not just to a specific tree frog.

Even though expository-informational books are not stories, they can still be appealing. For example, *The Life and Times of the Peanut* (Micucci, 1997) deals with a subject that is quite interesting to most young children. This 32-page book typically features a 2-page spread with a short passage on a topic related to peanuts:

> Three Thousand Years of Peanut Butter
>
> Each year, Americans eat more than 800 million pounds of peanut butter. Most of it is eaten by children. But American children were not the first peanut butter eaters.
>
> Almost 3,000 years ago, South American Indians ground peanuts into a sticky paste. Their peanut butter was not as spreadable as modern peanut butter and it tasted different, too. They mixed their gooey delight with cocoa, the main ingredient of chocolate. (p. 20)

Surrounding these paragraphs are attractive illustrations related to the history of peanut butter, each with a sentence or two of explanatory text.

Mixed Text: Combining Narrative and Expository Text

Many informational books combine narrative and expository writing. Although a number of terms have been used to describe these books, such as *dual-purpose*, *fuzzy*, *blended*, and *hybrid*, we use the term *mixed text*.

An example of a mixed text is *The Popcorn Book* (dePaola, 1978), which tells a story of twin brothers making popcorn. As they do so, one brother reads aloud facts about popcorn from an encyclopedia. All the text occurs in voice bubbles, but different type faces are used for the facts versus the story.

Another example of mixed text is the original Magic School Bus series. In *The Magic School Bus: Inside the Human Body* (Cole, 1990), readers follow the story of an imaginary teacher and her class as they take a trip. Surrounding the story are facts contained in boxes, charts, student reports, and illustrations showing lists and labels. (Note: The newer series based on the television episodes of the Magic School Bus differs from the original book series. The television-based series features narrative-informational books such as *The Magic School Bus Wet All Over: A Book About the Water Cycle* [Relf, 1996].)

Some Cautions About Narrative-Informational Text and Mixed Text

We recommended earlier that half the classroom library comprise informational books. Now we add to that recommendation by suggesting that narrative-informational or mixed texts make up no more than a third of those informational books. This means that most of the informational books in the class library would feature expository writing. As we explained, we believe this is a good idea because young children typically get more exposure to narratives. In addition, there are particular problems that are more likely to occur with narrative-informational or mixed texts than with expository-informational text.

One potential problem is that the story takes precedence over the factual information. With mixed text, such as many of the Magic School Bus books, some children may simply read the story and skip the factual portion. Jetton's (1994) research with a narrative-informational book illustrates this problem. Jetton had second graders listen to *Dear Mr. Blueberry* (James, 1991), a story that includes science concepts about whales. Half the children were told they would be listening to a story about a little girl who likes whales; the other half were told they would be listening for interesting facts about the life of whales. Regardless of the purpose, the children in both groups focused on the story ideas rather than the factual information.

Another problem is that narrative-informational books may lead inadvertently to misconceptions such as objects taking on human qualities. In a book such as *I Am a Leaf* (Marzollo, 1998), children may be misled by the anthropomorphism as they read, "Hi! I'm a leaf. I live on a maple tree. See the lady bug? She's crawling on me. It tickles!" (n.p.).

The younger the children, the more difficulty they may have telling fact from fiction. This problem is illustrated in Brabham, Boyd, and Edgington's (2000) study in which second, third, and fourth graders were engaged in read-alouds of two narrative-informational books. In *Everglades* (George, 1995), a Native American storyteller gives children historical and scientific information as he takes them on a canoe trip in the Florida Everglades, and in *Call Me Ahnighito* (Conrad, 1995), an anthropomorphic meteorite named Ahnighito tells his story. Children at all three grade levels showed some confusion, but the second graders had much more difficulty sorting the facts from the fictional elements and were more likely to attribute anthropomorphic characteristics to the meteorite.

To help avoid such problems, teachers should choose narrative-informational books with care (see chapter 3 for more information on choosing books). For example, as the excerpts from *The Emperor's Egg* and *I Am a Leaf* show, some authors are better at avoiding anthropomorphism than others. In addition, some authors take care to let readers know what is factual and what is conjecture. In *Bard of Avon: The Story of William Shakespeare* (Stanley & Vennema, 1992), for example, the authors include comments such as "No one knows when he left [Stratford for London]" (n.p.), and "Perhaps he allowed his five-year-old son, William to sit in front with him for the special performance. If so, it was the first play he ever saw" (n.p.). Some authors include notes that detail fact and conjecture; for example, in *Betsy Ross* (Wallner, 1994) readers are told,

> We know many facts about Betsy Ross's life, but there are also many conflicting stories. Some historians suggest that she won contests for her needlework. Others say she did not.... There is no absolute proof that Betsy Ross sewed the first American flag. The story...was passed down by Betsy's relatives and friends. (n.p.)

Similarly, unlike many biographies with invented dialogue, the picture book *Abraham Lincoln* (Cohn & Schmidt, 2002) includes only utterances for which there is historical evidence: "Leading a nation at war was the hardest task of all his life. People died, too many to count. President Lincoln grieved for each one. 'Sometimes I think I'm the tiredest man in the world'" (n.p.).

Sutherland, Monson, and Arbuthnot (1981) argue that

> Information can and should be written in a straightforward fashion; young readers need no palliative with books on science or geography or nature study. No "Mother Nature knew it was springtime" is admissible in children's nonfiction books, nor does a squirrel need to be referred to as "Little Nutsy." Children don't like to be talked down to. They can take information straight, although they can be bored stiff if the writing is too dry or too heavy. (p. 445)

This sentiment was echoed by one child who looked over a narrative-informational book and commented, "Oh, I know what this is. It's one of those fact books trying to pretend it's a story." If a book is that obvious, then it is probably not a successful one.

Fortunately, there are lots of excellent informational books for young children—including expository text—that are wonderfully appealing. This means that teachers can find good expository-informational books for their libraries. We provide many examples throughout this book.

Taking an Inventory of the Classroom Library

To be sure that children have the opportunity to experience the full range of the reading experience, it is important to inventory the classroom library. By taking stock of the content of the classroom library, teachers can decide how to achieve a better balance of fiction and informational text.

Inventorying Books

Two examples from ongoing research (Dreher & Baker, 2003) show how inventories can help teachers set goals for improving their libraries. One inventory of a third-grade classroom library, containing a large number of books, shows that most of the books are fiction (see Table 1). Only 22% are informational books and, of those, less than half are expository. After the teacher examined the results of her inventory, she decided to add informational books, particularly those that feature expository text.

The second inventory shows a second-grade classroom library with a similar pattern (see Table 2). Informational books make up a much smaller percentage of the collection than fiction (17% vs. 80%, respectively). But the underrepresentation of informational books is more problematic because there are fewer total books than in the

TABLE 1

Third-Grade Classroom Library Inventory

		Reading Level						
Type of Book		1st and Below	Low 2nd	High 2nd	Low 3rd	High 3rd	4th and Above	**Total**
Fiction		85	206	169	73	29	20	582 (74%)
Informational Book	Expository-Informational	3	22	17	13	12	4	71 (9%)
	Narrative-Informational	8	36	31	11	6	3	95 (12%)
	Mixed	0	2	1	0	2	0	5 (1%)
Other (Poetry, Jokes, Music)		4	11	9	7	0	0	31 (4%)
Total		100 (13%)	277 (35%)	227 (29%)	104 (13%)	49 (6%)	27 (3%)	784 (100%)

TABLE 2

Second-Grade Classroom Library Inventory

Type of Book		Reading Level: 1st and Below	Low 2nd	High 2nd	Low 3rd	High 3rd	4th and Above	Total
Fiction		6	63	29	14	5	2	119 (80%)
Informational Book	Expository-Informational	0	3	2	1	2	3	11 (7%)
	Narrative-Informational	2	2	6	2	1	0	13 (9%)
	Mixed	0	0	1	0	0	0	1 (1%)
Other (Poetry, Riddles)		0	1	3	0	1	0	5 (3%)
Total		8 (5%)	69 (46%)	41 (28%)	17 (11%)	9 (6%)	5 (3%)	149 (100%)

third-grade library. Thus, students have less opportunity to experience informational books.

These two examples parallel research findings that if there is a classroom library, it is typically mostly fiction. Thus, many teachers will find that inventorying their libraries will lead them to seek out more informational books for their classrooms. As they do so, we believe teachers should emphasize expository-informational books rather than narrative-informational books or mixed texts because young children need more exposure to expository text, and because of the cautions we have raised about narrative-informational and mixed books. As we suggested earlier, narrative-informational or mixed texts should make up no more than a third of the informational books in the classroom library. That way, if the classroom library is about half informational books, as we recommend, then most of those informational books will allow children to experience expository writing.

Selecting a Range of Reading Levels

It is important to consider the reading level of books in a classroom library in relation to the reading abilities of the children who are using the library. Mismatches between reading abilities and book levels in a classroom library are not uncommon. Martinez, Roser, Worthy, Strecker, and Gough (1997) found that the proportion of lower level books in second-grade classroom libraries was smaller than the relative demand for those books. For example, in one classroom, lower level books made up only 24% of the class library, but those books made up over 60% of what the children chose to read during the school year.

Tables 1 and 2 also show the reading levels of books in the classroom libraries. Both classrooms are in Title I schools with a very high percentage of minority students from low-socioeconomic-level families. Both include highly capable readers but also many struggling readers. Thus, in the third-grade classroom, it makes sense that many of the books are at reading levels lower than third grade. In the second-grade classroom, 74% of the books are at the second-grade level. Given the students' reading levels in that class, the teacher may need to increase the number of lower-level books. Further, it is clear that both libraries could use more informational books at each reading level.

Providing a Suitable Number of Books

How many books should a classroom library have? Based on a review of research, Fractor et al. (1993) concluded that a basic classroom library should include at least one book for each child, a good library should include at least four books for each child, and an excellent library at least eight books for each child. In an IRA position statement (1999), a similar conclusion was reached: "Given that there are approximately 180 days in the school year, a child should be able to select within the classroom a new book to read each day. This averages to about seven books per student in each classroom library" (n.p.). These figures should include multiple copies of some titles so that children can sometimes read a book at the same time as a classmate.

In the previous examples (Tables 1 and 2), the first classroom, with 25 children, has more than 30 books per child, while the other classroom, with 21 students, has 7 books per child. Both libraries would meet IRA's recommended number of books. In terms of number of books, the first library would rate *excellent* according to Fractor et al. (1993), while the second would rate *good*.

However, numbers alone do not tell the whole story. If books are dated, dull, worn out, unappealing, or at the wrong levels, they are unlikely to be read. Thus, books in the library need to be evaluated (see chapter 3). And as IRA (1999) recommends, "one new book per student should be added to every classroom library...each year to allow for the addition of important new titles and the elimination of books that are no longer timely" (n.p.). In addition, effective classroom libraries need to be well designed, as we discuss later in this chapter.

Moving Beyond Books

Classroom libraries benefit from resources other than books to promote children's engagement with print. These resources include listening stations with earphones; flannel boards, puppet theaters, and related props; magazines and newspapers; and Internet resources. We focus on two categories of print resources that offer young children ample opportunities to interact with informational text: (1) magazines and newspapers and (2) the Internet.

Children's Magazines and Newspapers

Children's newspapers are perfect additions to a classroom library. Not only do they offer children the chance to read informational text, they also provide up-to-the-minute information on current events in a way that children can understand. Similarly, magazines designed for young children also add to the classroom library's appeal. Children's magazines that feature informational text help to extend children's knowledge of the world. Like informational books, newspapers and magazines appeal to children's curiosity, which is strongly related to reading activity (Baker & Wigfield, 1999). There are several children's magazines and newspapers that feature informational text, many of which have websites with extension activities for teachers and children (see Appendix A, page 118).

Using Internet Resources

Not only are there many resources available online for young children, but digital technologies are highly appealing to children (Leu, 2002). Thus, if possible, computers and Internet access should be included in the classroom library. This will expand children's opportunity to interact with informational text because the content on Internet sites, including those for younger children, has been found to be mostly informational text (Kamil & Lane, 1998). Teachers should be aware, however, that even on sites intended for younger students, the reading level is typically higher than conventional expository-informational books at the intended grade levels (Kamil & Lane, 1998).

Teachers also should consult their school's policy on Internet use regarding requirements for adult supervision and monitoring of Internet usage. However, even if an adult is present, bookmarking good sites will help limit accidental access to inappropriate sites. Bookmarks also help make children's use of the computer more efficient. (See chapter 6 for examples of teacher-constructed webpages that organize websites for children.) Good candidates for bookmarking are the following search engines and directories that screen out sites inappropriate for children.

Ask Jeeves for Kids

www.ajkids.com

Children can use natural language to type in questions.

KidsClick!

http://sunsite.berkeley.edu/KidsClick!

This site is maintained by the Ramapo Catskill Library System.

Yahooligans

www.yahooligans.com

Sites are selected for ages 7–12.

Obtaining Resources for a Classroom Library

At this point, it must be evident that creating an excellent classroom library involves expense. All too often teachers pay for classroom libraries out of their personal income. To help remedy this situation, professional organizations have called for increased spending on books for the school and for classroom libraries (e.g., IRA, 1999). Continuing advocacy for library funding is needed. In the meantime, we provide a few ideas for expanding the classroom library.

Evaluate Existing Budgets

Budgets are always tight, but if classroom libraries are valued, then funds can sometimes be reallocated. Teachers may find it helpful to demonstrate the effectiveness of classroom libraries. For example, a kindergarten teacher in an urban school conducted an action research study to examine the effects of establishing a classroom lending library on her students and their parents (Britt & Baker, 1997). The children took turns staffing the library themselves and took great pride in doing so, with parents often coming to school to observe on the days their children were in charge. The project was very effective in promoting parent involvement and home-school communication. The principal was so impressed with the results that she allocated funds so that each classroom could start its own lending library.

Rotate Books From the School and Public Libraries

One good way to expand classroom libraries is to check out books from the school library or public library. This helps bring ever-changing titles into the classroom collection. If the school library is undersupplied, then it may be particularly important to draw on the public library. Many public libraries offer special teacher cards, with extended loan periods and a printout of titles to help with tracking.

Obtain Grants, Donations, and Discounts

Local newspapers, businesses, civic groups, and professional organizations often make small grants to schools for worthy projects. Schools can request funds for trade books to support literacy. Teachers can propose a project that helps obtain funds for expanding the classroom library. For example, the State of Maryland IRA Council encourages classroom-based research by offering small grants, typically in the range of $250. Many other IRA state councils offer similar grants. Such programs may help fund a well-conceived project to involve children with books.

Another way to supplement the classroom library is to maintain a wish list of books and magazine subscriptions. That way, if parents give gifts to teachers for holidays or teacher appreciation day, they can select items from the wish list. At some schools, parents donate a book from the wish list for their child's birthday. In addition, the wish list can guide donations from the Parent Teacher Association or other organizations that wish to help the school.

Bookstore discounts and sales also are helpful. Many bookstores offer substantial discounts for teachers, often increasing the discount on designated teacher-appreciation days. Further, warehouse and Internet sales can greatly reduce prices. For example, Scholastic holds sales with deep discounts at its warehouses nationwide. Dates and locations of sales are posted on Scholastic's website (http://teacher.scholastic.com/fairs/warehouse) where teachers can sign up for e-mail alerts.

Include Student-Produced Books

Books written by the children in a classroom are important additions to the classroom library. Young children enjoy creating both single- and group-authored books, and they enjoy reading and rereading their own and one another's books. When second graders each contributed pages to an informational book as part of an inquiry unit, the book was among the most popular in the classroom library (Korkeamäki, Tiainen, & Dreher, 1998).

In one first-grade class, the children write class books all year long and add these books to the classroom library. These books are so loved that the children are eager to own one. At the end of year, the class holds a lottery for the student-produced books: Each book is assigned a number, the children pick numbers out of hat, and the winners get to take home the book with the corresponding number.

Creating an Appealing Classroom Library Environment

The physical environment of the classroom library makes a difference in its appeal to children. Morrow (1991) has summarized her own and others' research showing that much more than the number of books influences a library's effectiveness. Features like size, accessibility, arrangement of furniture, open-face shelving, organization, variety of genres, ease of checking books in and out, and regular influx of new books are all important. In fact, Morrow found that redesigning the classroom library can make it a highly appealing center that entices children to spend more free time reading.

Thus, research makes it clear that well-stocked, well-designed libraries should be the goal in every classroom. Specifically, Fractor et al. (1993) concluded that in addition to lots of books, an excellent classroom library should be set off from the rest of the classroom with partitions or shelves. It should have a name, be quiet and well lit, and offer seating or carpeting for at least five children at a time. Books should be displayed face out, in an organized way. Further, the library should include materials such as puppets, flannel boards, or costumes that encourage children to reread or engage in books in other ways.

We suggest that all teachers strive for an excellent classroom library. We provide a checklist (see Appendix B, page 128) that teachers can use to evaluate their progress toward library excellence.

Managing the Classroom Library

To make a library work, teachers need to set up a good management system to keep order. There should be a simple method for checking books in and out, a plan for organizing the books, and a place to put books that need repair. Teachers do not have to manage the libraries alone. Not only can primary-grade children help out, they enjoy doing so. A special benefit of involving children in managing the library is that it adds to their feeling of ownership.

Library-related roles can be some of the class jobs. Children as young as kindergarten age can operate a simple method for checking books in and out (Britt & Baker, 1997). Children can also be in charge of identifying books that need repair and placing them in a book first-aid corner. They also can help keep the books in order. For example, if teachers code books with colored stickers that match their placement in the library, even young children can sort and arrange the books.

Time to Read

Recently, a second-grade teacher and her class received some new books as a gift for helping with a project. As these books were presented, the class was told that they were for the classroom library. A young girl spontaneously expressed her frustration, complaining, "We never use our library!" (Dreher & Baker, 2003).

This anecdote helps to illustrate an important point: A well-designed library can be a major contributor to helping children become eager and competent readers, but only if children have time to use it: Access to books involves not only having the books but also having time to read them (IRA, 1999).

Summary

By providing easy access to books and other print material, classroom libraries can help children become skilled and motivated readers. Classroom libraries should include an equal balance of fiction and informational text. Further, the informational text should include a high proportion of expository writing because primary-grade children typically have much less exposure to this type of writing than to narrative forms. By evaluating their classroom libraries, teachers can determine any changes that need to be made in order to provide students with highly appealing centers. But if the library is to be successful, teachers must provide time for children to use it. In addition, "Without the support of teachers who introduce the materials and feature books in daily routines, the physical factors alone will not succeed" (Morrow, 1991, p. 687). In the following chapters, we will provide many ideas to help introduce and feature informational books. In chapter 3, we will discuss how to choose quality books for classroom use, while the remaining chapters offer instructional suggestions to enhance children's learning from informational text.

CHAPTER

3

Choosing Informational Books for the Classroom

There is a wealth of good informational books available to the primary-grade classroom teacher. Publishers now, more than ever before, are producing colorful, attractive, interesting informational books designed for primary-grade children. However, among these books, some are better than others, and it is up to the teacher to choose appropriate ones for the classroom. Several aspects should be considered when making book choices such as accurate content, appealing design and format, engaging writing style, and good organization.

Accurate Content

Perhaps the most important feature of an informational book is the accuracy of its content. By its very nature, an informational book is written to inform and enlighten; if information is inaccurate, the book fails in its primary goal.

Although "accurate content" is an easy concept to state, in reality, it is much harder to define. As children's author Russell Freedman (1992) has posted above his keyboard, "Something can be perfectly accurate but untrue" (p. 4). Authors not only have the responsibility to gather facts but also to present them in a balanced, responsible way so that truth is not compromised.

Each time an author writes a book, especially for primary-grade readers, she must decide what to include and what to omit. These decisions form the basis for the essential truth of an informational book. Authors (and illustrators) should strive to present information that will satisfy a child's curiosity about a topic while including all known (or theorized) information that is appropriate for the child's developing level of understanding.

The evidence is clear that children learn from reading and looking at informational books (Mayer, 1995; Pappas, 1993; Rice, 2002; Smolkin & Donovan, 2001); therefore, it is crucial that the information presented to them is accurate. Authors and illustrators must be very careful not to mislead through text or pictures. For example, children reading *The Mixed-Up Chameleon* (Carle, 1975) can mistakenly assume from the illustrations that chameleons can change to colors other than greens and browns (such as white, yellow, or red). Children viewing the illustrations in *Terrible Tyrannosaurs* (Zoehfeld, 2001) can mistakenly believe that dinosaurs lived at the same time as humans because one illustration shows a dinosaur looking into a second-floor bedroom and another shows a dinosaur standing beside a truck. Mayer (1995) reported that children who listened to *Dear Mr. Blueberry* (James, 1991), featuring letters written between a young girl and a scientist about whales, actually came away from it with misconceptions. Instead of remembering the accurate details given by Mr. Blueberry, the children remembered the misconceptions held by the girl that were shown in the illustrations. Further, as Rice (2002) points out, children reading the otherwise excellent book *The Reason for a Flower* (Heller, 1983) can learn incorrectly from the text that mushrooms are plants.

As mentioned in chapter 2, authors should be careful to indicate the differences between what is known and what is believed or suspected to be true. When discussing theory that has not yet been proven, an author should indicate this through the use of words such as *scientists think,* or *scientists believe*. In *Terrible Tyrannosaurs*, the author is careful to ensure that the reader is aware of the lack of certainty about dinosaurs:

> But T. Rex's skull can tell us even more. Inside was room for a brain that was the largest of nearly all the dinosaurs. Scientists think this big brain must have endowed T. Rex with extremely keen senses. Perhaps it could catch the scent of a duckbill herd, or hear the low footfall of Triceratops, from miles away. (p. 20)

In determining whether content is accurate, it is useful to consider the credentials of authors and the references they use. Often, this information can be found on the book jacket, at the end of the book, or on the verso of the title page. If an author is not a specialist on a topic, subject experts are often listed as having assisted the author or having reviewed the manuscript. Sometimes an author will list print sources as well. For example, in *Biggest, Strongest, Fastest* (Jenkins, 1995), the following three of five reference books are listed on the verso of the title page, which may indicate that the information in the book is accurate:

> Bateman, Graham (ed). *Children's Encyclopedia of the Animal Kingdom*. New York: Dorset, 1991;
>
> Buchsbaum, Ralph, et al. *The National Audubon Society of Animal Life*. New York: Clarkson N. Potter, 1982; and
>
> Morris, Rick. *Mysteries & Marvels of Ocean Life*. London: Usborne Publishing Limited, 1983. (p. ii)

Special care is needed in examining books about multicultural groups. Generally, those individuals who are part of a particular cultural group—*insiders*—can speak with more authority than those outside the cultural group—*outsiders*. It is possible, however, for an outsider to have enough familiarity with a culture to portray it accurately. Again, sometimes if an author does not seem to be an insider, consultants may be listed to assure that the information is accurate. For example, in *The Hopi* (Lassieur, 2002), the Hopi Literacy Project and the Bureau of Applied Research in Anthropology at the University of Arizona are listed as consultants. In any book representing minority cultures, care should always be taken that stereotypes are not used, either in text or illustration.

An additional component of accurate content is how current the information is. It is important that the most up-to-date information be included in books about science, but it is equally as germane for books reflecting newly independent nations or discussing minority cultures. In many instances, outdated informational books may not include all that is known about a topic or may contain information that has been proven false or may include stereotypes indicative of the time they were written. Therefore, it is always important to check a book's copyright date.

However, although a copyright date may be recent, it does not guarantee that the information is current. For example, in *Breakfast Around the World* (Perez, 2000), a map of Germany shows only West Germany, yet East and West Germany reunited in 1990. Additionally, sometimes a book's copyright date reflects the publishing date by the current publisher—not the date the book was written. For example, *Spiders* (Cullen, 1996), which has a copyright date of 1996, was first published in Australia in 1986.

As Rice (2002) notes about children's science books, "Errors of omission, incomplete statements, value statements, outdated information, and lack of detail create problems just as overtly erroneous information does" (p. 563). However, Rice also points out that teachers can continue to use books that contain inaccuracies as long as they are aware of them. In fact, pointing out errors or conflicting information can encourage children to become critical readers who question the accuracy of what they read.

It is important, therefore, for teachers to carefully examine books that they are planning to use with their classes—identifying potential problems, misunderstandings, and misconceptions—and to develop ways to help children use books effectively in spite of any shortcomings. One second-grade teacher reported, "I can make any book work!" (Dreher & Voelker, in press). To make a book work in the classroom, however, a teacher must be able to spot the possible problems and design compensatory lessons. This might be as simple as pointing out to children that although a picture shows a dinosaur looking in a second-story window in *Terrible Tyrannosaurs*, this could not happen because there were no people or houses during the time that the dinosaurs lived.

Appealing Design and Format

No matter how accurate books are, if they are not visually appealing to children, the books are not likely to be read. Many recently published informational books are richly designed and visually attractive. Nonetheless, there are particular aspects of design that add to a book's value. The design of the book needs to reinforce the content.

Illustrations and text should be placed appropriately on pages. Books for primary readers, especially, should have text and illustrations placed in such a way that children are not confused about which part to read first if sequence is important. Although some informational books have text that does not read from left to right and is presented in circles or in other formats (e.g., see Figure 2), older readers can usually understand these, and the unusual formatting actually adds to the interest of the book. However, beginning readers, reading independently, need to have text that reads from left to right and from the top to the bottom of the page. Teachers can show beginning readers how to read books with alternate designs through read-alouds (see chapter 4).

Illustrations in informational books may be photographs, diagrams, maps, drawings, charts, or figures. Illustrations can represent and clarify information and can extend the information in text. For example, in *Growing Vegetable Soup* (Ehlert, 1987), illustrations are used to specify what isn't spelled out in the text. The text reads, "We're ready to work, and our tools are ready, too," and the illustrations explain what the tools are—a shovel, a rake, and a hoe. Often, captions can be

FIGURE 2

Example of Unusual Print Format

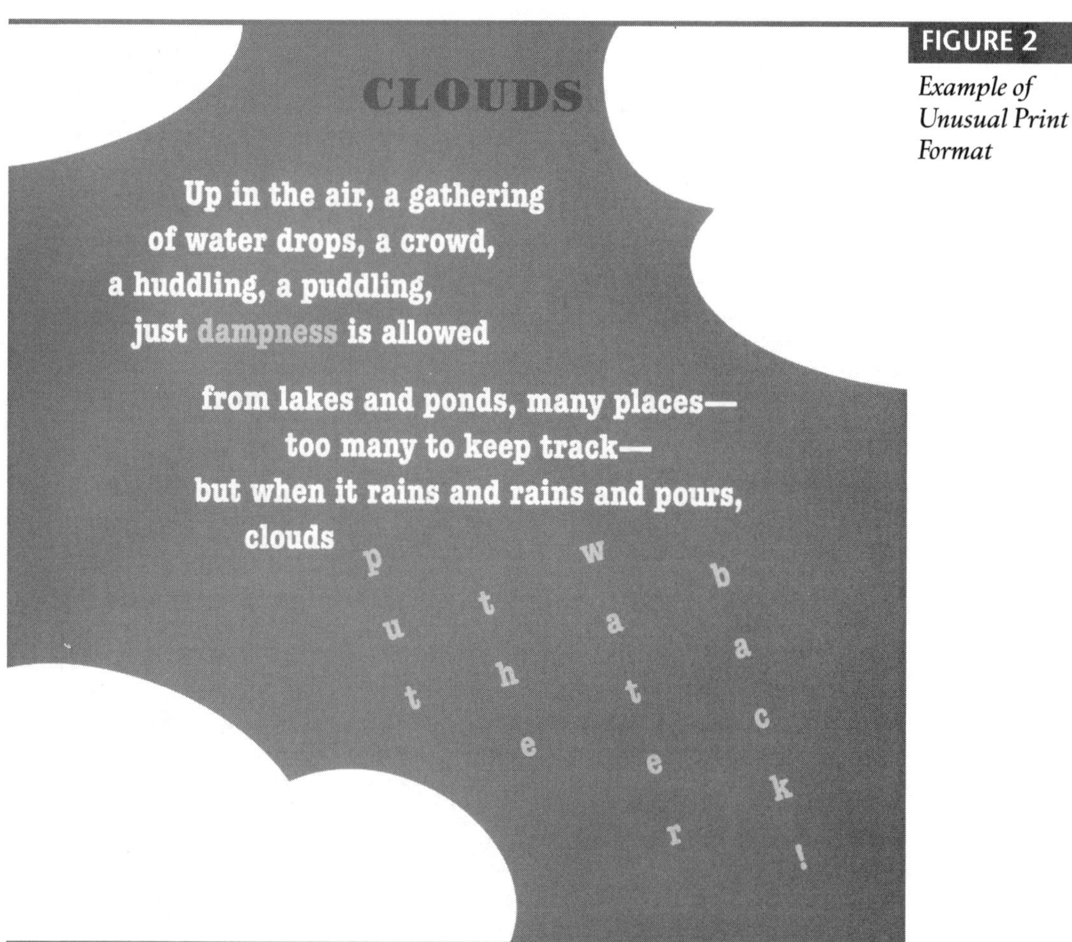

CLOUDS
Up in the air, a gathering
of water drops, a crowd,
a huddling, a puddling,
just dampness is allowed
from lakes and ponds, many places—
too many to keep track—
but when it rains and rains and pours,
clouds
put them water back!

From Splish Splash. *Text copyright © 1994 by Joan Bransfield Graham. Reprinted by permission of Houghton Mifflin Company. All rights reserved.*

used to add additional information to the text. In *I Love Guinea Pigs* (King-Smith, 1994), the captions provide more specific information about guinea pigs than is in the actual text of the book (see Figure 3).

In some books, illustrations do not support the text as well as they might, and children may have difficulty understanding either the text or the illustrations. For example, the text in *Bugs Are Insects* (Rockwell, 2001) discusses the fact that all insect bodies are divided into three parts, but it is difficult to tell from the attractive illustrations where the three body parts are located. Labeling the parts would have made them clear to children and teachers. Similarly, *Body Numbers* (Looye, 1998)

FIGURE 3

Example of Information in Captions

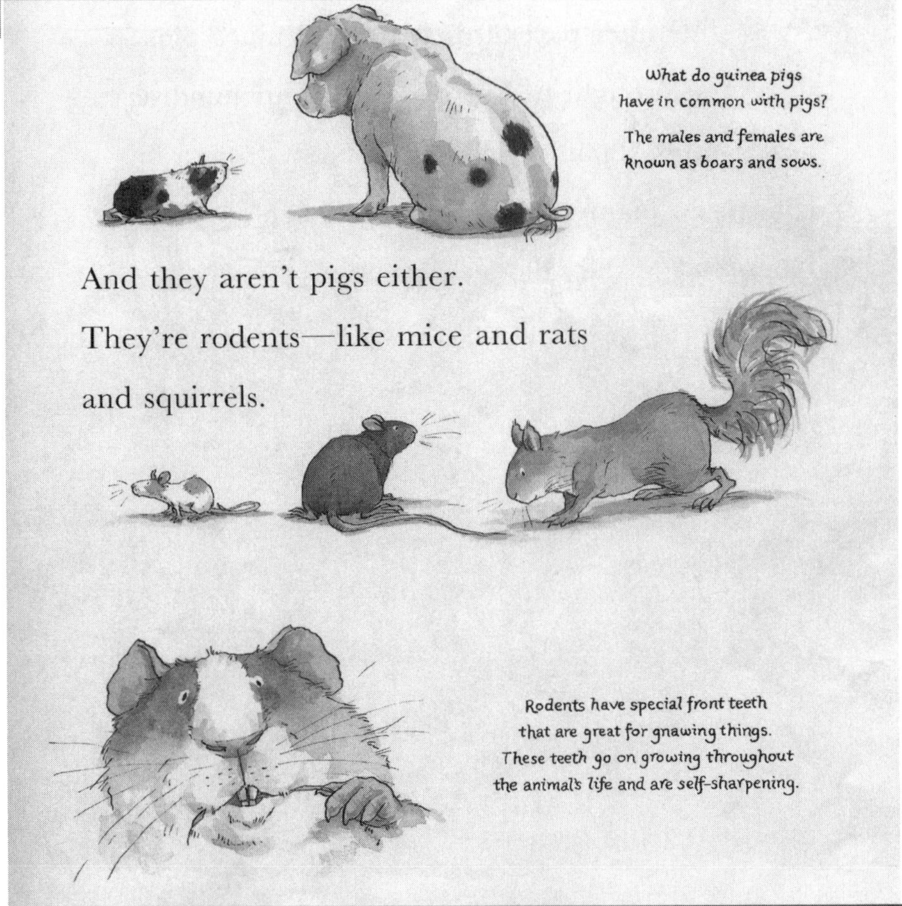

What do guinea pigs have in common with pigs?
The males and females are known as boars and sows.
And they aren't pigs either.
They're rodents—like mice and rats and squirrels.
Rodents have special front teeth that are great for gnawing things. These teeth go on growing throughout the animal's life and are self-sharpening.

From I Love Guinea Pigs *by Dick King-Smith. (1994). Text © 1994 by Foxbusters Ltd. Illustrations © 1994 by Anita Jeram. Reproduced by permission of Candlewick Press, Inc., Cambridge, MA, on behalf of Walker Books Ltd., London.*

contains text that explains that the human heart has four chambers; however, the illustration provided does not indicate the chambers, which makes it impossible for children or teachers to get a mental picture of a heart chamber based on the text or illustration.

Captions should be placed close to illustrations and provide clear explanations. If illustrations are maps or graphs, they should be clearly labeled. In *Bugs Are Insects* (Rockwell, 2001), the illustrations lose effectiveness because the identifying information for each is listed on the book's last page. Teachers and children who are trying to identify the insects in the book constantly must turn to the back to consult the list. Additionally, the insects discussed in the text are not presented from left to right as would be expected.

Illustrations should be appropriate for the content of the book. For example, the pen-and-ink drawings used to illustrate the somewhat challenging book *Cathedral* (Macaulay, 1973) fit perfectly with the architectural content of the book (see Figure 4). Likewise, the

FIGURE 4

Example of Illustration Matching Content

From Cathedral: The Story of Its Construction. *Copyright © 1973 by David Macaulay. Reprinted by permission of Houghton Mifflin Company.*

expressive drawings in *Duke Ellington* (Pinkney, 1998) complement the lively text and Ellington's music (see Figure 5).

Many informational books use photographs to clarify or expand the text. When photographs are used, it may be important to know the origin of photographs in order to judge their accuracy. In *Galaxies*

FIGURE 5

Example of Illustration Mirroring Content and Style

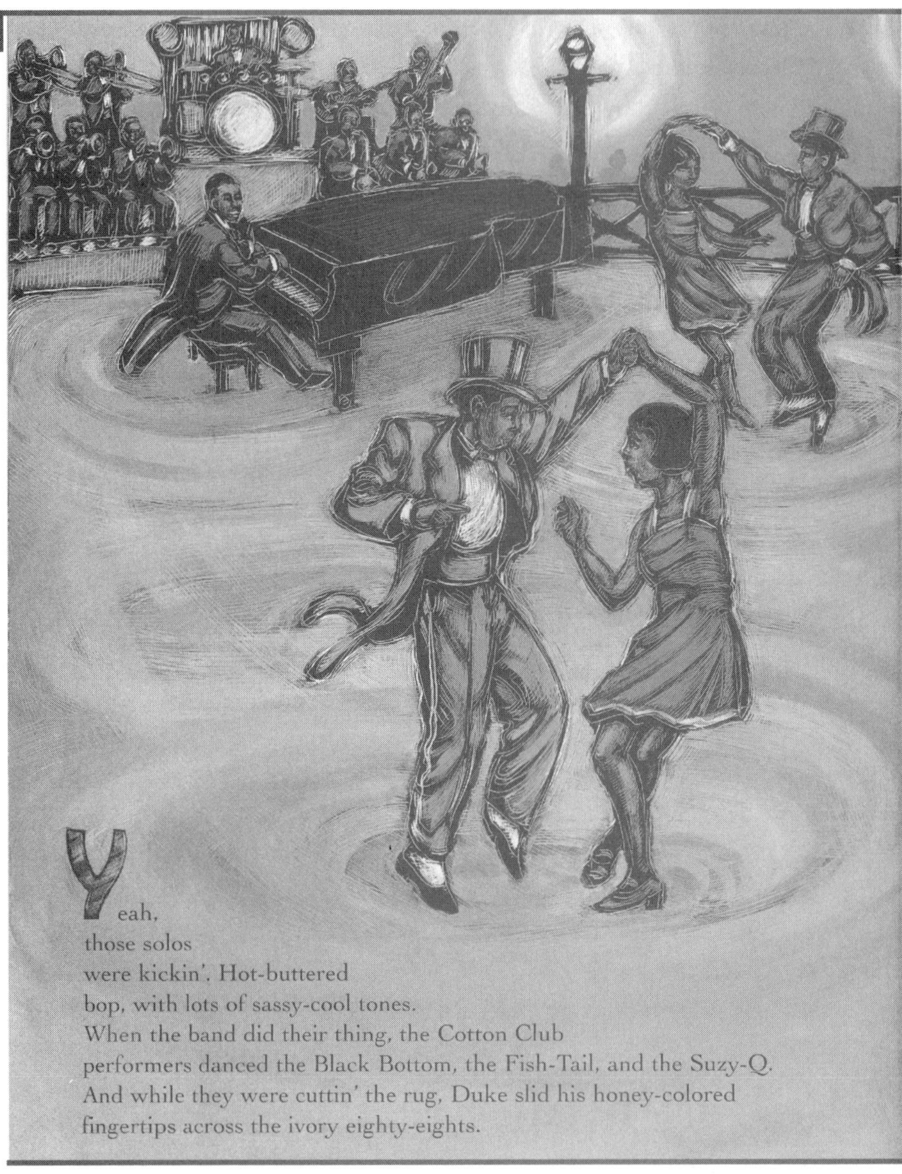

Yeah,
those solos
were kickin'. Hot-buttered
bop, with lots of sassy-cool tones.
When the band did their thing, the Cotton Club
performers danced the Black Bottom, the Fish-Tail, and the Suzy-Q.
And while they were cuttin' the rug, Duke slid his honey-colored
fingertips across the ivory eighty-eights.

From Duke Ellington *by Andrea Davis Pinkney (1998). Illustrations copyright © 1997 by Brian Pinkney. Reprinted by permission of Hyperion Books for Children.*

(Simon, 1988), for example, the photo credits list the National Optical Astronomy Observatories on the verso of the title page.

For many books, it is important that illustrations indicate relative size. For example, in *How Big Were the Dinosaurs? Gigantic!* (O'Brien, 1999) drawings of dinosaurs are placed next to well-known objects to indicate their relative size. In *Biggest, Strongest, Fastest* (Jenkins, 1995), small illustrations are used throughout the book to indicate the animals' size (and strength) relative to humans (see Figure 6). These illustrations enable children to compare new information about the animals to known information about humans.

It is also important for books to indicate when photographs have been enlarged so that children can understand the difference between a close-up or magnified view and a normal view. In the book *Spiders* (Cullen, 1996), for example, the author indicates when the drawing has been magnified by placing the word "enlarged" after the caption for pictures that are close-ups.

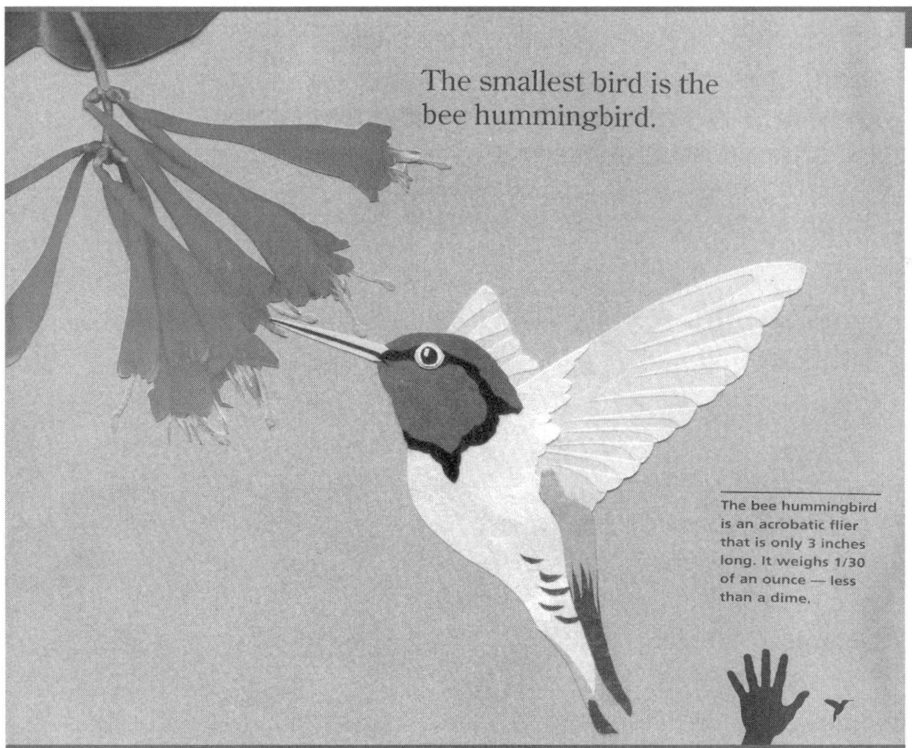

The smallest bird is the bee hummingbird.
The bee hummingbird is an acrobatic flier that is only 3 inches long. It weighs 1/30 of an ounce — less than a dime.

FIGURE 6

Example of Illustration Showing Relative Size

From Biggest, Strongest, Fastest. *Copyright © 1995 by Steve Jenkins. Reprinted by permission of Houghton Mifflin Company. All rights reserved.*

Engaging Writing Style

The best informational books have lively, engaging language with the author's voice in evidence. At the same time, appropriate terminology is important. Part of the content of a good informational book is the introduction of the language of the topic. For example, in *Monarch Butterfly* (Gibbons, 1989), the terms *larva*, *molting*, *chrysalis*, *pupa*, *abdomen*, and *metamorphosis* are introduced. Likewise, an appropriate term such as *photosynthesis* is used in *Leaves* (Saunders-Smith, 1998). As Pappas (1993) documents, kindergarten children are quite capable of learning correct terminology with repeated readings of informational books. They should have the opportunity to do so.

Authors who write with enthusiasm for their subjects invite children to share in their wonder. Frequent use of second-person "you" in books often serves to draw children into the text. Use of comparisons, language with cadence and rhythm, and active verbs can make the text engaging. In *Under New York* (High, 2001), the author captures the rhythm of New York City with language:

> Under New York,
> below taxicabs and tour buses and carriage horses,
> there are railroad tracks and trains whizzing past,
> clattering fast,
> bringing visitors to the city and taking them home again. (n.p.)

The best informational books do not present only collections of facts; they also develop concepts and generalizations about topics. Young readers should come away with a general understanding of the topic as well as specific factual information. In fact, the best books are those that are organized thematically with specific factual detail supporting the themes.

Slap, Squeak & Scatter: How Animals Communicate (Jenkins, 2001) provides a good example of a thematically organized book with supporting factual detail. The entire book describes how animals communicate and focuses on the different purposes for communication in the animal kingdom. These purposes are printed at the top left-hand page in yellow on a black background. For example, "Many animals communicate to warn one another of danger. When every member of a group watches out for predators, they are all more likely to survive" (p. 3).

These generalizations are followed by illustrations and examples of specific animals' communication patterns that warn of danger. An illustration is shown of a beaver with the following text at the bottom of the page: "A beaver that detects danger will warn other beavers by slapping its tail on the water with such force that the sound can be heard half a mile away" (p. 3). On following pages, Jenkins explains how the vervet monkeys, the white-tailed deer, and the chaffinches warn others of danger. Children who read this book will understand the generalizations as well as the specific information about individual animals.

Good Organization

Choosing informational books with good organization is important because children need to experience typical expository patterns and informational book features. Expository patterns, such as *cause-effect, comparison-contrast, sequence, question-answer, description,* and *generalization-example* (Meyer, Brandt, & Bluth, 1980) are characteristic of informational text. For example, *Bears* (Merrick, 2000) is written with a question-answer format, while *Arctic Foxes and Red Foxes* (Meadows & Vail, 2002) follows a comparison-contrast format. For children to learn to use these patterns to guide their comprehension (see chapter 5) or use them in their own writing (see chapter 7), they must have experience with them. Therefore, it is important that teachers choose books with clear organizational patterns often indicated by headings and subheadings.

Unlike stories, much informational text does not have to be read from beginning to end, and children need to learn this important concept. Children should have informational books available that exemplify features that can be used to find information quickly that will satisfy their curiosity. Books such as *The Hopi* (Lassieur, 2002)—with a table of contents, glossary, map, an index, useful addresses, Internet sites, and a list of other books to read—can help children explore these book features. In chapter 6, we discuss specific ways in which teachers can help children learn to use these features.

Some informational books, however, do need to be read from beginning to end. Books explaining topics that are sequential, such as the life cycle of butterflies or the water cycle, need to be read in order.

Other books may need to be read from beginning to end because of the repetition and rhyming of the language. Children need to experience all these different organizational patterns.

A Guide for Choosing Informational Books

To help teachers evaluate informational books, we have developed a guide (see Appendix B, page 129), which they can use to identify particular characteristics of books and to decide which books will be valuable in their classroom libraries and in their teaching. Using the guide also can alert teachers to particular problems that they and their students may encounter with a particular book. Once the teacher is aware of these problems, she can plan activities to be sure that children are able to learn successfully from the book.

A guide developed for *Polar Bears* (Gibbons, 2001) summarizes this book's many valuable features for teachers to use in instruction (see Figure 7). For example, as noted in the guide, the book's illustrations are clear and introduce vocabulary that is important to the study of polar bears. By using the illustrations, teachers can show children both how to read diagrams in informational books and help them learn the new words presented there. On the other hand, there is nothing in the book to indicate whether or not an illustration is an enlargement, which can create possible confusion for children. By using the guide to evaluate the book in advance, teachers can be aware of potential problems and can plan to explain which diagrams are enlargements.

Figure 8 shows a guide that was developed for a more challenging book, *Wild West* (Murray, 2001). This book, too, has many valuable features that would make it a good instructional tool. For example, it presents many primary sources that a teacher could use to introduce children to the concept of primary and secondary sources. On the other hand, some of these primary sources contain stereotypes of cultural groups, such as Native Americans and African Americans, which reflect the times in which they were written; therefore, the teacher would need to make children aware of the misrepresentations. By using the guide to think through these issues in advance, teachers will be better prepared to develop lessons that focus on a books' positive features and to avoid possible problems.

FIGURE 7

Guide for Choosing Informational Books: Polar Bears

Name of Book <u>*Polar Bears* (Gibbons, 2001)</u> Type of Book <u>Expository-Informational</u>

Characteristic	Notes	Possible Instruction
Content Accuracy		
Author's and illustrator's qualifications • Experts in field • "Insiders" (if multicultural book) • Award-winning	Gail Gibbons, author of many informational books	Connect to *Ducks!*, which children have already read
References used • Consultants who are experts • Print sources	Thanks James Doherty, General Curator at NY Zoo Society	Show children where to find what experts have contributed to book
Information current • Copyright date recent (if important) • Information up to date	Copyright 2001	
Distinguishes between fact and theory • Clear what is believed and what is known	Uses "scientists believe" when discussing nonproven facts	Point out to children that this phrase means we don't know for sure
Text and illustrations clear	Yes	
Stereotypes not used in text or illustration	N/A	
Design		
Illustrations appropriate for content	Yes, drawn	Point out to children that drawings can be used in an informational book as well as photos
Illustrations well placed on the page • Clear about where to begin reading	Yes, though there is reading in the drawings too	Show children the difference in typeface between text and illustration explanations
Illustrations labeled and explained	Yes, a lot of additional information and terminology in the illustrations	Use illustrations for vocabulary instruction as well as how to read diagrams

(continued)

FIGURE 7

continued

Characteristic	Notes	Possible Instruction
Captions clear and informative	Captions placed within the illustrations	
Relative sizes indicated • Enlargements noted	No	Explain to children that some of the drawings are close-ups; point out which ones
Style		
Lively, engaging language	Yes	
Accurate terminology used	Yes	Useful for teaching vocabulary related to polar bears
Appropriate for children's level	Some sophisticated concepts for first grade	Use additional explanation for difficult concepts
Generalizations and concepts given (not just a collection of facts)	Connections made and facts used as illustrations of important points	
Enthusiasm for topic evident	Yes	
Organization		
Informational book characteristics • Pagination, table of contents, index, glossary, additional reading list	No pagination, no table of contents, no index, no glossary, no additional reading list; additional facts listed at end of book	Could be used for children to generate table of contents, index, and glossary Difficult to use for searching for specific information
Headings and subheadings	Only one heading—"polar bear characteristics" (somewhat misleading)	Could be used for children to generate headings (as in table of contents)
Clear pattern of organization	Must be inferred; mostly description	Could be used to help children infer organization

FIGURE 8

Guide for Choosing Informational Books: Wild West

Name of Book *Wild West, Eyewitness Book* Type of Book Expository-Informational

Characteristic	Notes	Possible Instruction
Content Accuracy		
Author's and illustrator's qualifications • Experts in field • "Insiders" (if multicultural book) • Award-winning	Stuart Murray, in collaboration with the Smithsonian Institution	Introduce children to the Smithsonian and to the Eyewitness series
References used • Consultants who are experts • Print sources	Consultants from the Smithsonian National Museum of American History and the National Postal Museum	
Information current • Copyright date recent (if important) • Information up to date	2001	
Distinguishes between fact and theory • Clear what is believed and what is known	Presents most information as factual	Could use to help children understand about primary sources
Text and illustrations clear	Much of the information is included in the text with the illustrations	
Stereotypes not used in text or illustration	Illustrations taken from the Smithsonian; some use stereotypes to illustrate historical record	Good opportunity to talk about stereotypes and why people might have used them
Design		
Illustrations appropriate for content	Yes	
Illustrations well placed on the page • Clear where to begin reading	Illustrations well placed; appropriate to begin reading in many different places	Children need experience in distinguishing text from illustration captions; point out differences in typeface

(continued)

FIGURE 8

continued

Characteristic	Notes	Possible Instruction
Illustrations labeled and explained	Most information is in the explanation of the illustrations	Children need to know that they have to read the captions to understand the points being made
Captions clear and informative	Yes, containing much information	
Relative sizes indicated • Enlargements noted	No	Children need to be made aware of this
Style		
Lively, engaging language	Yes	
Accurate terminology used	Yes	Can be used for vocabulary development
Appropriate for children's level	Challenging even for third grade	Use parts as read-aloud
Generalizations and concepts given (not just a collection of facts)	Generalizations in text with illustrations providing examples and factual information	Children may need help in discovering the generalizations
Enthusiasm for topic evident	Yes	
Organization		
Informational book characteristics • Pagination, table of contents, index, glossary, additional reading list	Table of contents, index, pagination; no glossary or additional reading list	Good for table of contents and index instruction
Headings and subheadings	No; chapter titles are like headings	
Clear pattern of organization	Not sequential; can be accessed at any page; mostly description	Good for showing children how to find specific information

Sources for Quality Informational Books

Fortunately, numerous sources are available online to help teachers identify good quality informational books (see Appendix A, page 122). Print journals also offer much information. For example, the Children's Choices and Teachers' Choices annual lists of popular story and informational books are published by the International Reading Association in *The Reading Teacher* in October and November, respectively, and also are available as separate booklets.

Since 1990, the National Council of Teachers of English (NCTE) has presented the Orbis Pictus Award for Outstanding Nonfiction for Children each year to an excellent informational book. Winners, honor books, and recommended titles are available from NCTE. The Association for Library Services to Children presents the Robert F. Sibert Information Book Award to the author of the most outstanding informational book published in the United States during the year. The Caldecott and Newbery Medals honor authors and illustrators for both storybooks and informational books. Lists of these award-winning books are available from the American Library Association.

The list Outstanding Science Trade Books for Children is published in the March issue of National Science Teachers Association's (NSTA) *Science and Children* and provides annotations of books and recommended grade levels for their use. Similarly, the National Council for the Social Studies (NCSS) in cooperation with the Children's Book Council publishes Notable Children's Trade Books in the Field of Social Studies in the April/May issue of *Social Education*. This list, divided into social studies themes, includes both storybooks and informational books. Annotations and recommended grade levels are provided for each book.

The Horn Book, published six times a year, and *Book Links: Connecting Books, Libraries and Classrooms*, published eight times a year, are good sources for identifying excellent informational books. These magazines include annotations of books and suggestions for how to use them in classrooms.

Summary

There are many good informational books available to the primary-grade teacher. It is important to choose them carefully for inclusion in classroom libraries and for reading and content area instruction. Even if books have a few shortcomings, teachers can use them effectively with the proper planning. In the following chapters, we will describe how teachers can use these books for read-alouds, comprehension instruction, teaching search strategies, and writing instruction.

CHAPTER

4

Using Informational Books for Read-Alouds

There is widespread agreement that teachers should regularly read aloud to children (IRA/NAEYC, 1998; Snow, Burns, & Griffin, 1998). Reading aloud is widely recommended because it leads to increased reading achievement, promotes independent reading, and supports struggling readers. Rosenhouse, Feitelson, Kita, and Goldstein (1997), for example, found that at-risk first graders improved in decoding, reading comprehension, and storytelling ability when their teachers interacted with students before, during, and after reading a story. We also know that read-alouds in school increase children's vocabulary (Elley, 1989) and, if teachers have read a book aloud, children are more likely to select it during free reading time than other books in a classroom library (Martinez, Roser, Worthy, Strecker, & Gough, 1997). Further, when teachers read a book to their students, they provide scaffolding that makes the book easier to approach for struggling readers (Fielding & Roller, 1992).

Why Informational Books Make Good Read-Alouds

Although evidence indicates that most read-alouds are fiction (Hoffman, Roser, & Battle, 1993; Jacobs, Morrison, & Swinyard, 2000), teachers can and should include informational books. One reason to include them, as discussed in chapter 1, is that informational books deal with interesting topics, and interest is an important part of intrinsic motivation to read. Reading aloud informational books inspires curiosity in children, and for some struggling readers, informational books may hold the key to learning to read. With appealing topics, interesting formats, and great illustrations, informational books draw in children. As one second grader commented, "You know that book about whales? We learned so-o-o-o much about them. I was wondering if you could bring some other books like that I can read about countries...like Mexico" (Dreher & Dromsky, 2000).

Another reason to read aloud from informational books is that it helps children to learn linguistic features that differ from stories. For example, unlike stories, expository-informational books often use general statements and timeless verb construction, for example, "Tree frogs have sticky fingers and toes" (Royston, 1991, p. 10). In a classic study, Pappas (1993) showed that kindergartners performed just as well when asked to pretend to read informational books as they did with storybooks. They were able to adopt the distinctive language of each genre. Duke and Kays (1998) found that at the beginning of the year, kindergartners already were sensitive to differences between storybooks and informational books. But when children experienced three months of almost daily read-alouds of informational books, they showed even more skill with the distinct linguistic features. Duke and Kays concluded that informational book read-alouds resulted in "fast-developing knowledge of information book language" (p. 295).

Other studies of the primary grades, including many in urban classrooms with at-risk children, have shown similar results (Pappas & Barry, 1997; Pappas, Varelas, Barry, & O'Neill, 2000). Primary-grade children respond well to interactive reading of informational books, learning book language, and easily making intertextual connections among the books they read (Oyler & Barry, 1996).

In addition, informational book read-alouds offer a rich venue to support comprehension. In studies with first graders, Smolkin and Donovan (2001) found that read-alouds of informational books resulted in many more comprehension-related responses (i.e., interpreting, telling, personal association, literary association, elaborations, predictions, and wondering) than did storybook read-alouds. In one first-grade classroom, 70% of children's responses as they interacted with informational books were comprehension related, while only 30% of responses during storybook read-alouds were comprehension related. In another first-grade classroom, comprehension-related responses were 78% and 22%, respectively, for informational books and stories. Thus, informational book read-alouds seem to promote much interaction centered around meaning seeking.

An Equal Balance in Read-Alouds

We recommend that teachers read aloud every day and aim for an equal balance of fiction and informational text. Just as we recommended in our discussion of the classroom library (see chapter 2), we believe that if children are to become equally proficient with both fiction and informational text, they need the opportunity to experience both types of text (Dreher, 2000), and we suggest that teachers make an effort to include expository-informational books as a substantial part of their informational read-alouds. If most informational book read-alouds are expository-informational, then young children have the opportunity to learn about that type of writing. This experience will help children as they read such books on their own and when they are asked to write informational text (see chapter 7).

Teachers can work toward a 50/50 balance of fiction and informational text by examining their current read-aloud patterns. When Dreher and Dromsky (2000) asked two second-grade teachers to keep track of their daily read-alouds, they found that one teacher chose to read stories 84% of the time, while the other read stories 79% of the time. The high percentage of stories indicates that both teachers need to add more informational text to their read-alouds. However, they also need to examine the kind of informational text they choose because many of the informational books they read contain narrative writing. For example, during one month, one teacher read 16 books to her class. Although three of the books were informational text (biographies), they were narrative-informational books. This means that all the read-alouds that month were narratives; the children did not experience any expository text.

Using Read-Aloud Logs

To help diversify read-aloud selections, we suggest that teachers keep a log of what they read that includes not only the date, author, and title but also the type of book (see Appendix B, page 131). By including the type of book, teachers can quickly determine the balance of fiction and informational books they are reading to students. To avoid relying heavily on narrative-informational books, we have included separate columns for each type of informational book.

The read-aloud log can be modified as needed. In addition to subcategories for informational books, for example, teachers could include subcategories for types of fiction they wish to highlight. Whatever the final form, a read-aloud log serves as a visual record of all the books read. It can be posted in the classroom so that children can see which books their class has read and how many. Displaying the log also makes intertextual references easier because children can consult the log to refresh their memories of titles and authors they liked.

Teachers can involve students in filling out the read-aloud log. Helping to record read-alouds can be motivating for children because it helps them to see just how many books their class has read. It also can be a learning experience for students as they develop their sense of the characteristics of each type of book by helping to decide which columns to check.

Pairing Fiction and Informational Read-Alouds

One way teachers can get started in diversifying their read-alouds is to pair fiction with informational books. For example, a teacher who reads the classic story *Frog and Toad Are Friends* (Lobel, 1979) might also read *Amazing Frogs & Toads* (Clarke, 1990), an informational book with wonderful photos and fascinating facts. Similarly, *Little Bear* (Minarik, 2003), another classic story, could be paired with *Bears* (Kalman & Everts, 1994), which is filled with factual information about and beautiful photos of real bears.

Although pairing fiction and informational books is not a new suggestion (e.g., Sanacore, 1991), it has taken on more urgency with the current emphasis on helping children learn to handle informational writing. In a recent article, Camp (2000) put a new spin on pairing texts by calling it "teaching with Twin Texts" (p. 400). Among her suggestions were to twin *The Foot Book* (Dr. Seuss, 1968) with *What Neat Feet!* (Machotka, 1991), and *Cloudy With a Chance of Meatballs* (Barrett, 1978) with *Comets, Meteors, and Asteroids* (Simon, 1994). Pairs like these can help teachers feel comfortable with informational read-alouds. But, of course, it is not necessary to pair every title, particularly as informational book read-alouds become second nature.

Read-Alouds From the Content Areas

Some primary-grade teachers select many of their read-alouds based on their science, math, and social studies units. They report that reading aloud books related to content area units helps them to maximize their time and that their students enjoy the books. Evidence suggests that tapping content area units for read-alouds may not only boost children's knowledge but may also motivate them by activating their curiosity. For example, when Pressley and his colleagues (2003) studied primary-grade teachers, one characteristic they noted was that highly motivating teachers often integrated science, math, and social studies content into literacy instruction.

Books such as *Dinosaur* (Walker & Gray, 2001) from the Dorling Kindersley's Eye Wonder series or *Prehistoric Record Breakers* (Theodorou, 1998) from Rigby's Discovery World series are sure to be popular read-alouds that extend a unit on dinosaurs. Similarly, a book such as *Lightning* (Kramer, 1992) would not only be a high-interest read-aloud, it would complement a unit on weather. To identify likely books for a particular unit, teachers can consult their media specialist, as well as the many sources discussed in chapter 3. Also, content area teachers' manuals and curriculum guides often include suggested read-alouds.

Read-Alouds From Magazines and Newspapers

Another way to diversify read-alouds is to occasionally read magazine or newspaper articles that relate to class themes or concerns. Children's magazines and newspapers (see Appendix A, page 118) offer good sources for articles. In addition, many local and national newspapers include a children's section; for example, the *Washington Post* "KidsPost" contains current events and feature articles for children (www.washingtonpost.com/kidspost).

Read-Alouds Can Help Support Struggling Readers

Throughout elementary school, children's listening comprehension is typically better than their reading comprehension (Sticht & James, 1984). This means children can listen to read-alouds—both stories and informational books—which they would not be able to read independently. This seems particularly important for teachers to keep in mind for struggling readers who often are not interested in the books that they can read independently. Reading aloud informational books on appealing topics that otherwise might be too difficult can help extend children's knowledge and maintain their motivation.

When teachers read aloud from books that may be a bit difficult, they provide children with the knowledge and familiarity needed to tackle a book that is "too hard" on their own. Interestingly, Donovan, Smolkin, and Lomax (2000) documented this pattern in a recent study. They found that less proficient readers will select and read informational books—even books that are theoretically too hard for them—in a classroom in which the teacher does a lot of reading aloud. The support and prior knowledge from having heard the book, along with the high interest in the topic, may enable this to occur. Of course, as we previously noted (see chapter 2), it also is important that the classroom library has plenty of books that match the independent reading levels of struggling readers.

The Importance of Interactive Read-Alouds

To maximize the effectiveness of read-alouds, we suggest that teachers make them interactive. This means that children engage in discussion during the read-aloud by asking questions, offering suggestions, and making interpretations. In contrast, however, many teachers report they were taught to read a book all the way through with no discussion.

Yet the interaction during a read-aloud makes a difference, as Horowitz and Freeman (1995) found when they investigated the effect of discussion on kindergartners' and second graders' preferences for an expository science book or a narrative-informational science book. With no discussion, the children preferred the narrative-informational book. But with discussion, they preferred the expository science book even though they recognized that it contained more words they did not know.

Interactive read-alouds differ from read-alouds that follow an I-R-E pattern in which a teacher Initiates, students Respond, and teacher Evaluates. Interactive read-alouds are less teacher controlled, with children initiating and responding during the reading. When children ask questions, offer suggestions, and discuss one another's interpretations, this interaction engages children in meaning seeking and motivates them to read.

Children appear to benefit more from interactive read-alouds than from a teacher-controlled I-R-E pattern or from read-alouds with no discussion. When Copenhaver (2001) studied read-alouds in which there was little or no discussion or with a tightly controlled I-R-E pattern, she concluded that "all students were negatively affected by the limited opportunities to respond and the small range of ways in which to deliver their responses" (p. 151).

In contrast, with interactive read-alouds, Oyler (1996) found that in an urban high-poverty school, first graders actively contributed to the discussion. The children initiated a variety of book talk ranging from questioning for understanding to personal experiences to intertextual links. These interactive read-alouds allowed children to contribute their own knowledge to the discussion and to become critical readers who questioned "the teacher, the text, and each other" (p. 157).

For many teachers, interactive read-alouds will mean making changes. The first-grade teacher whom Oyler studied noted that in moving to interactive read-alouds, "She had to take risks to give up control, to let it flow, to let the predictions, questions, intertextual links, and other kinds of initiations emerge in ongoing reading/discussion around books" (Pappas & Barry, 1997, p. 231). But doing this did not mean she was giving up authority. As Oyler (1996) observed, the teacher "jumped in to correct misconceptions; she chose her read-alouds with careful attention to genre, language, and theme; and she played an active role in negotiating her students' initiations and understandings" (p. 158).

Different Ways of Reading Informational Books

As with storybooks, some informational books need to be read from beginning to end. This is often the case in narrative-informational books. For example, the story format of the *Emperor's Egg* (Jenkins, 1999; see chapter 2) means that it needs to be read from beginning to end. Many expository books for young children also are best read from beginning to end. For example, although *Zipping, Zapping, Zooming Bats* (Earle, 1995) does not have a story line, neither does it have a table of contents, an index, or headings that would help readers to determine where they might want to begin reading the book if they did not want to read from beginning to end.

In contrast, many informational books are arranged so that readers can begin on any page. In *Prehistoric Record Breakers* (Theodorou, 1998), each page deals with a different dinosaur. During a read-aloud, teachers and children could consult the list on the contents page and read in any order they choose. In *Bears* (Kalman & Everts, 1994), headings such as "What's for dinner?" "Where do bears live?" and "Bears in danger" clearly mark each section and are listed in the table of contents. There also is an index from which children could choose a topic of interest. These features allow read-alouds to proceed according to children's interests. In addition, by modeling the use of these features during read-alouds, teachers can show children how to search for information, as we describe in chapter 6.

Many books for young children now incorporate nontraditional designs, with information arranged across the pages in ways that do not conform to designs children usually encounter when they are learning to read. Books such as *Exploring Freshwater Habitats* (Snowball, 1994) and the Eye Wonder and Eyewitness Junior series (e.g. *Reptiles*, Taylor & Holland, 2002; *Amazing Flying Machines*, Kerrod, 1992) display topics on two-page speads with large and small photographs and drawings accompanied by related facts (see Figure 9). Designs such as these are increasingly popular in children's trade books (Moss, 2001) and also are encountered in textbooks (Walpole, 1998/1999). Children can begin reading such books on almost any page and almost anywhere on a page.

Reading aloud books with nontraditional designs allows teachers to help students learn how to approach them. In order to instruct children about these books, teachers need children to sit close enough to see the details, which may mean reading in small groups or using Big Books when available. Another technique is to use a document camera—similar to an overhead projector—that can display opaque objects as well as transparencies. The camera is hooked up to a television monitor or LCD (liquid crystal display) projector and allows teachers to zoom in and out on a book's pages to help children see exactly what is being discussed. Thus, nontraditional book designs may require teachers to alter their read-aloud techniques.

FIGURE 9

Example of Nontraditional Book Design

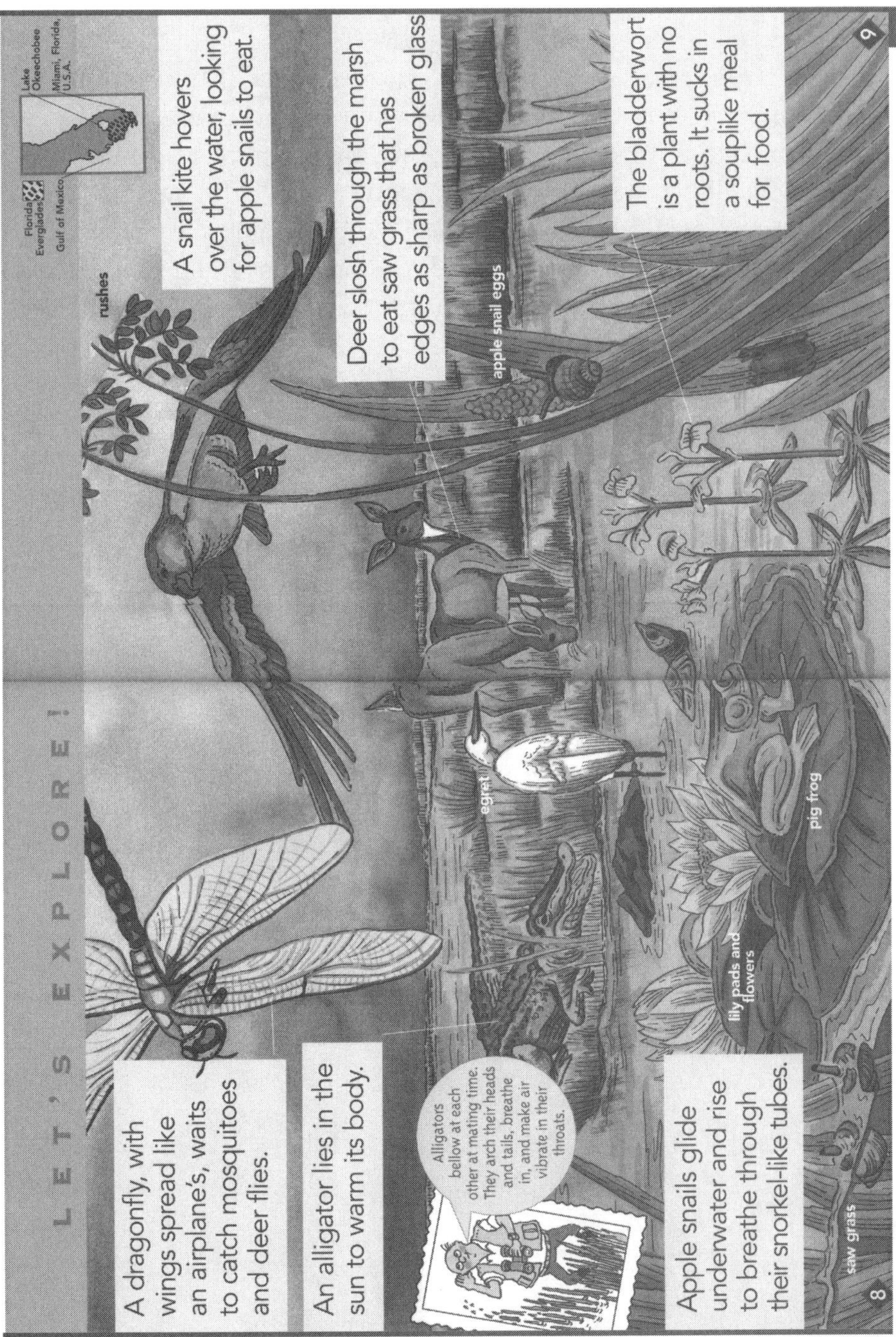

From Exploring Freshwater Habitats *by Diane Snowball. Wildlife illustrations by Cynthia A. Belcher. Cartoon illustrations by Miriam Katin from Mondo's BOOKSHOP® Literacy Program.*

Summary

There is strong evidence that read-alouds are valuable to children's achievement and motivation. Teachers should read aloud regularly from good books. Although research and longstanding tradition support reading fiction, there is also good reason to include informational text. Informational books offer rich potential for inspiring curiosity and learning, and reading them aloud is a great vehicle for teaching comprehension strategies and content knowledge, as we show in chapter 5.

CHAPTER

5

Teaching Comprehension Strategies Using Informational Text

Comprehension—constructing meaning from text—depends on readers' conscious or automatic use of comprehension strategies. Teaching students strategies to help them comprehend is important—even for students who are still developing word-level proficiency (Pearson & Duke, 2002; Snow, Burns, & Griffin, 1998). Children who learn comprehension strategies in the early years will become stronger, more capable readers, who are better able to cope with more advanced texts.

We know that strategies can be taught effectively when the teacher explains directly what the strategy is, how to use it, and when it is appropriate (Duffy, 2002). Explaining the strategy can be followed by teacher modeling, guided practice for the students, and gradual release of responsibility to the students for carrying out the strategy on their own (Pearson & Duke, 2002). However, this sequence is far from being a rigid plan to follow in strategy instruction. As Duffy (2002) explains, "Success depends on thoughtfully selecting and then adapting techniques that fit the situation" (p. 38). Success requires that teachers know what the strategies are and when they are appropriate, recognize when the students are ready to learn them, and help students learn to be strategic. Ideally "teachers and students act as a literary community, using strategies to construct and evaluate interpretations of text" (El-Dinary, 2002, p. 202).

Certain reading comprehension strategies are particularly useful in reading informational text and, therefore, are best developed using these texts (see Figure 10). The most useful strategies for informational text are accessing prior knowledge; predicting based on titles, headings,

FIGURE 10

Comprehension Strategies for Informational Text

Before Reading	During Reading	After Reading
Accessing prior knowledge	Making connections	Summarizing
Predicting	Questioning	Creating pictures and graphs
Questioning	Visualizing	
	Inferencing	
	Using text structure to identify major ideas	
	Paraphrasing	
	Clarifying	

and pictures; inferencing; questioning; visualizing; using text structure to identify major ideas; making connections; and summarizing (Kletzien, 1991). These strategies can be used before, during, and after reading. (Note that we use the term *strategy* for what the readers themselves do to construct meaning. In this book we do not use the term *strategies* to refer to techniques, such as DRTA [Stauffer, 1975] or K-W-L [Ogle, 1986] that teachers use as part of their lessons.)

Strategies can be introduced one at a time so that students can understand specifically what the strategy is, how it can be done, and when it is appropriate. The eventual goal is to enable the students to learn to "be strategic" rather than simply to know a lot of strategies. This means that students need to be able to orchestrate a group of strategies, knowing which ones are appropriate for any given task or text, knowing how to choose among the strategies they know, and knowing when the strategies will be useful (Brown, Pressley, Van Meter, & Schuder, 1996; NICHD, 2000). Although this may seem like a daunting task for primary-grade readers, learning to be strategic can be supported through read-alouds as well as through instructional reading groups. This will give young readers ample opportunity to work with being strategic even before they are proficient at decoding. Van den

Broek and Kremer (2000) make the argument that for beginning readers, many of the important reading strategies can be taught even before children are reading; in fact, it may be easier for them to learn these strategies in settings that do not require them to decode.

A suggested plan for strategy instruction (see Appendix A, page 124) is to introduce a text by talking to the children about the topic to access their prior knowledge. Then, if it is the first time a strategy has been introduced, provide direct instruction in what the strategy is, how it is done, when it is appropriate, and why it is useful. Next, model using the strategy with the chosen text, gradually having children join in using the strategy as they read the text. Discuss using the strategy throughout the text and then review at the end of the lesson what the strategy was, how the children used it, when they might use it again, and how it helped them.

It is important to provide ample practice for the strategies following the initial lesson. Children need to have scaffolded lessons in which the teacher gradually releases the responsibility for using the strategy to the children. This can be done by having children first work with the teacher, then work in pairs or small groups before being expected to carry out the strategies independently. As in most other learning tasks, some children will begin to use the strategies quickly whereas others will need additional practice before they can use them proficiently. It is vitally important, however, to have this practice within the context of real reading for meaning so that children will learn the importance of using strategies for comprehension. Using strategies in quest of comprehension in authentic reading situations will prevent the problem of having children who can perform a skill in isolation but cannot transfer it to reading situations.

Providing lots of practice in authentic contexts becomes easier as teachers realize that they can teach these strategies while working with content areas such as science and social studies. As children read these content area texts, they should always be encouraged to use the comprehension strategies that have been introduced. In this way, they are not only getting additional practice, but they are also having the opportunity to apply the strategies to new text for real purposes.

Once the strategies have been introduced, taught, and practiced, children can simply be reminded to use the strategies they know.

Children can even be asked which strategies they find appropriate for the text and the task before they read, and which ones they used after they have completed the reading. It is important to remember that strategy use is idiosyncratic; that is, what may work well for one individual may not work so well for another; what may work well for one text may not work well for a different text. It is important that children have opportunities to learn and practice multiple strategies, but they may use different ones while reading the very same text.

Before-Reading Strategies

Before reading a selection, teachers should activate students' prior knowledge, assess what prior knowledge they have, provide any additional needed information, arouse curiosity, and motivate students to want to read. Strategies most likely to be useful before reading include accessing prior knowledge, and predicting based on title, headings, and pictures. Using informational text, teachers can introduce and model each of these strategies.

Accessing Prior Knowledge

To introduce the idea of accessing prior knowledge before reading, a second-grade teacher chose to read *Ducks!* (Gibbons, 2001). First, she showed the cover of the book to the children and explained to them that before they start reading about a topic, they should think about what they already know about it. She told the students that this would help them to be active readers who think about what they are reading and notice whether the text confirms or contradicts what they already know. She explained to the children that this is always a good idea when they are reading informational text.

Then, she modeled thinking about what she already knew about ducks. She mentioned seeing some ducks at the local pond where children were feeding them bread. She talked about the ducks' colors and the quacking sound they made. She listed these details on chart paper in front of the group. Then, she asked the children what they already knew or had heard about ducks and added these ideas to the chart paper. She intervened when one child contradicted something another one said by putting both ideas on the chart with question marks and telling the children to look for the information while they were reading.

As the teacher and children read *Ducks!* the teacher referred to the list on the chart paper. If a fact was confirmed, she invited a child to put a check mark next to it. When a fact was refuted, she corrected it. For example, one child had said that ducks live in the ocean, which the book confirmed; however, the book also added that ducks live on lakes and streams. The teacher corrected the chart to read, "Ducks live in the ocean and on lakes and streams."

At the end of the reading, the teacher directed students to look at the chart paper with their confirmed and corrected facts. She asked them how they could find out about the facts that were neither confirmed nor corrected. The children suggested various strategies such as reading another book, looking at the ducks in the zoo or at the local pond, or asking an adult. She asked them how thinking about what they already knew helped them to understand and remember the information.

The teacher encouraged the children to develop a strategy for independent reading by supporting their efforts to access their prior knowledge, showing them how to read to confirm or refute their ideas, and directing their attention to other ways of finding out information. Having the children reflect on how the strategy helped them increased their metacognitive awareness and made it more likely that they would use this strategy in the future.

Predicting

Predicting in informational books is different from predicting in stories. In stories, readers predict what will happen, that is, how the story will unfold, what the characters will do, and what the resolution will be. In informational books, predicting is used to think about what kind of information the author has probably included.

As a small group of second graders was introduced to *Slap, Squeak & Scatter: How Animals Communicate* (Jenkins, 2001), one teacher demonstrated the predicting strategy. First, he read the title and showed the children the cover of the book. Then he reminded them that good readers predict what a book is about before they read it. He invited the children to predict what kinds of information would be in the book. When the children seemed stuck, he modeled for them how to predict from the title:

> Let's see, well, it says how animals communicate, so I would predict that the author will tell us what the animals might want to communicate—maybe where there is food or maybe that there is danger. I guess he will also tell us how animals communicate because they don't talk the way we do. Because the title is *Slap, Squeak, and Scatter*, I predict that some animals may slap something to communicate, some might squeak, and I don't know what it would mean to scatter.

At this point, the children became engaged and began talking about which animals might squeak and which ones might slap. The teacher directed their attention to the other prediction: What might the animals be trying to communicate?

After a brief discussion, the students took a "picture walk" through the book, discussing the illustrations and adding to their predictions about what would be in the book. The teacher reminded them that predicting what will be in the book is a good way to be active readers and that they can always use this strategy with informational books.

As the group read the book, students checked their predictions, frequently commenting on particular information that they had predicted would be presented. At the end of the lesson, the teacher again reminded the students about predicting what information would likely be included in an informational book. He checked their understanding by holding up *Growing Up Wild: Wolves* (Markle, 2001). The children were encouraged to predict what kind of information might be included in this book. After a quick picture walk, during which time the children added to their predictions of the kind of information that would be included, the teacher added the book to the reading corner and suggested that the students check their predictions during independent reading time.

Clearly, children will be able to use prediction for information only if they have had experience with informational books. When Cathy Yost, a second-grade teacher in Pennsylvania, reads informational books with her children, she makes explicit comments about the kind of information that an author has included. When she begins a new book, she asks the children to predict what the author has included. For example, before reading *Hungry, Hungry Sharks* (Cole,

1986), she asked children what kind of information they would expect to find in the book. Children began predicting specific facts about sharks, and Cathy used the opportunity to make the statements more general. One boy suggested that they will find out that sharks eat fish. Cathy responded by saying yes, they will probably find out what sharks eat...maybe fish. After modeling this kind of response two or three times, the children began making general statements about what they expect to read such as "where sharks live." Cathy reminded the children that they have read other books about animals that have included similar information.

Each time teachers read informational books with their children, they can remind them of these strategies until the children use them without being prompted.

During-Reading Strategies

During reading, teachers want children actively engaging in reading, monitoring their comprehension, and connecting new information with what is already known. Strategies most likely to be useful during reading include questioning, using text structure, visualizing, inferencing, making connections, and clarifying.

Questioning

Questioning is a powerful strategy to use with informational text either before or during reading. When teaching students about questioning, a teacher might use a collection of informational books about a particular topic. For example, one second-grade teacher used a text set about bears to introduce children to the idea of questioning (see Figure 11). First, she reminded children to think about what they already knew about bears before beginning reading. Then she explained to them that asking questions is a good strategy to use before and during reading. It will help them be active readers by reading to find answers to their questions.

She modeled how to look at one or two of the book covers, think about questions she had, and write these questions on sticky notes. She placed the notes on the table in front of the children. Then she invited the students to page through the books and think about questions they had. As the students volunteered questions, she jotted them on sticky

FIGURE 11

Text Set for Bears

Berger, M. (1999). *Growl! A book about bears*. New York: Cartwheel.
Gibbons, G. (2001). *Polar bears*. New York: Holiday House.
Gill, S. (1992). *Alaska's three bears*. Ill. S. Cartwright. New York: Scholastic.
Greenland, C. (1985). *Nature's children: Black bears*. Danbury, CT: Grolier.
Greenland, C. (1986). *Nature's children: Grizzly bears*. Danbury, CT: Grolier.
Greenland, C. (1986). *Nature's children: Polar bears*. Danbury, CT: Grolier.
Hodge, D. (1997). *Bears: Polar bears, black bears and grizzly bears*. Ill. P. Stephens & N.G. Ogle. Tonawanda, NY: Kids Can Press.
Holmes, K.J. (1998). *Bears*. Minneapolis, MN: Bridgestone.
Kalman, B., & Everts, T. (1994). *Bears*. New York: Crabtree.
Markle, S. (2000). *Growing up wild: Bears*. New York: Atheneum.
Merrick, P. (2000). *Bears*. Chanhassen, MN: The Child's World.
Simon, S. (2002). *See More Readers: Wild bears*. New York: SeaStar.
Whitehouse, P. (2002). *Brown bear*. Portsmouth, NH: Heinemann.

notes and added them to the collection on the table. After many questions had been generated, she led the children into categorizing them. Identified categories included where bears live, what bears eat, and differences between types of bears. Some of the children's questions related to specific pictures in the book—such as "Why are these bears fighting?"—and thus did not fit into the categories. These questions were put into a separate group.

The teacher pointed out that informational books do not have to be read from beginning to end, but instead can be used to find answers to questions. She pointed to the questions about what bears eat and showed children the table of contents from *Bears* (Merrick, 2000) in which one chapter is titled "What Do Bears Eat?" She modeled for students how to read the table of contents to find the chapter about what bears eat and find the page where the chapter begins. (See chapter 6 for more information about how to teach children to use the table of contents and index.)

As students turned to the specific page and began reading, they found the answers to several of their questions. Each time students found an answer to a question, the teacher stopped them to make sure that they understood that the answer had been found. She then asked the students to put the sticky note with the question on the page that answered the question.

The teacher showed students that additional questions might be raised during reading. She put a stack of blank sticky notes on the table for children to use to add to their questions. She explained that they might need to read other books, magazines, or Internet pages to find additional information to answer their questions.

As these second-grade students used the text set to try to find answers to their other questions, they soon discovered that not all the books had tables of contents. The teacher helped them skim the pictures and text to search for clues to locate the information.

Using Text Structure

Most children have a fairly good grasp of story structure; that is, they expect to have characters, a problem, and a resolution. They may learn this through direct instruction or by countless hours of watching, listening to, or reading stories. Informational text structures, on the other hand, are more varied, and many children do not have the same experience with them as with stories. Yet we know that using text structure is an important part of being a strategic reader (Kletzien, 1992) and that understanding expository text structure can help children comprehend (Richgels, McGee, Lomax, & Sheard, 1987; Roller, 1990).

The most common text structures in informational writing are cause-effect, comparison-contrast, sequence, description, and problem-solution (Kane, 1998; Meyer, Brandt, & Bluth, 1980; see Appendix A, page 125). Books such as *Bears* (Merrick, 2000) use a question-answer structure that is also commonly found in informational books for children. *Slap, Squeak and Scatter* (Jenkins, 2001) follows another often-used structure: generalization followed by examples. Usually these structures have key words that signal when they are being used. Although teachers may want to wait until the intermediate grades for in-depth instruction on these structures, introducing some of them to primary-grade children will enable them to use the structures more proficiently later in reading and writing.

In addition to teaching children to notice key words that often accompany a particular structure, teachers can introduce graphic organizers to help them record information. Children can use a simple organizer for each structure to help them focus on the major ideas from selections and to raise their awareness of the overall structure of the text (Feldt, Feldt, & Kilburg, 2002). Appropriate graphic organizers are introduced individually as books with particular text structures are discussed. As a small-group or whole-class activity, children read a selection, identify the structure, and then fill in the appropriate organizer. In the following sections, we provide examples of these graphic organizers; these also can be used for writing summaries or reports (see chapter 7 for writing ideas).

Cause-Effect. Using a book such as *The Reasons for Seasons* (Gibbons, 1995) is a good way to introduce children to the cause-effect structure common in informational books. Although there is description in this book as well, the major structure is cause-effect. The author explains through text and diagrams what makes the seasons (see Figure 12).

FIGURE 12

Cause-Effect Graphic for The Reasons for Seasons

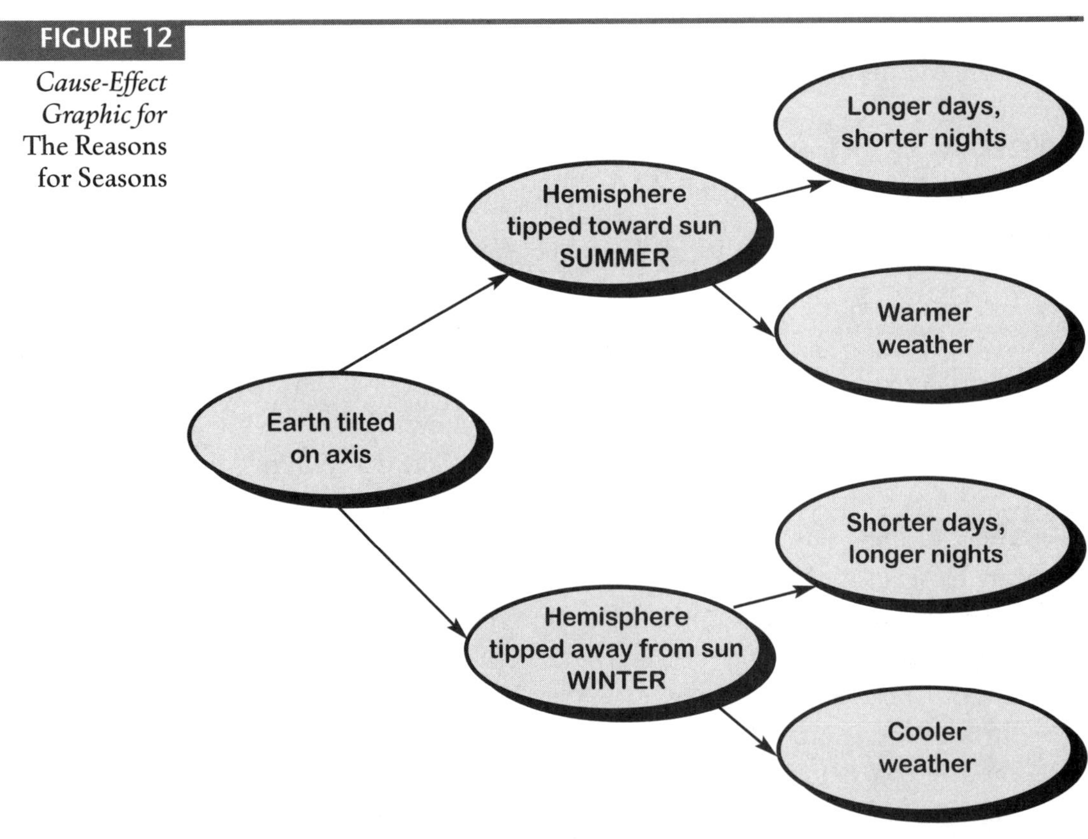

Comparison-Contrast. Using the math book *If You Hopped Like a Frog* (Schwartz, 1999), teachers can have children think about what they would be able to do if they had the abilities of different animals and insects. Many comparison-contrast books, such as *Wasps & Bees* (Meadows & Vail, 2003), are available about creatures that are often confused. A comparison chart or Venn diagram, both of which show similarities and differences, can be used to help children clarify their understanding of these animals' characteristics (see Figure 13).

Sequence. Many informational books are written in sequence. Most how-to books that give directions have this structure. For example, *How to Draw Trucks and Cars* (Smith, 1996) gives step-by-step instructions for drawing a number of different kinds of cars and trucks. In this particular book, the steps are numbered, making it easy for children to understand the idea of sequence.

Another example, *Milk: From Cow to Carton* (Aliki, 1974), begins with a cow eating grass and ends with pouring milk into cartons at the dairy. One way that teachers could make the sequence in this book more obvious to children would be to have them list the events in order or to create a timeline (see Figure 14). The author uses many typical sequence words such as *then* and *after* in this book.

FIGURE 13

Comparison Chart for Wasps and Bees

Wasps	Both	Bees
Thin waist	Found everywhere in the world	Thick waist
Few body hairs	3 pairs of legs	Thick coat of body hair
Most don't sting	1 pair antennae	All can sting
Wasps that sting use sting to kill prey and to protect themselves	Bodies have 3 parts	Use sting only to protect themselves
Wasps that sting can do so multiple times		Can sting only once

FIGURE 14

Sequence for Milk

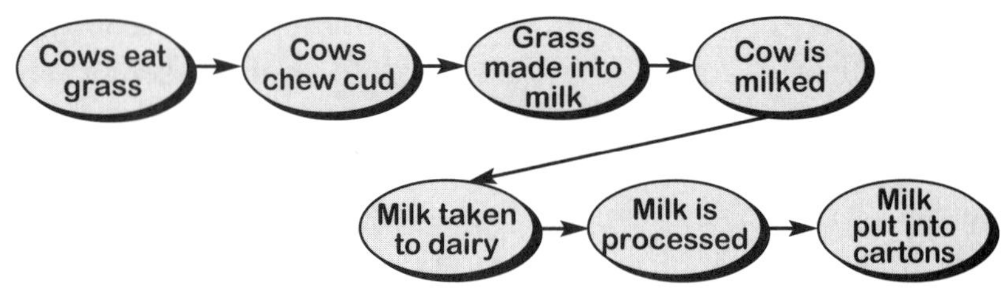

Description. The book *Dolphins* (James, 2002), written in a description structure, provides detailed information about what dolphins look like, what they eat, and where they live. A concept map would help children organize this information (see Figure 15). Because many books are written in a description structure, children should be encouraged to create concept maps showing how ideas are related. The resulting maps also can be used for writing summaries or reports (see chapter 7).

Children can be encouraged to look for examples of structures as they read informational text and will find many texts with multiple structures. For this reason, it is important not to insist on a single interpretation of what the text structure is; rather, encourage children to discuss which parts of the text represent different text structures. After children practice identifying these text structures, they can begin to use them in their own writing (see chapter 7 for ideas about writing).

Other During-Reading Strategies

Similar lessons can be developed to introduce other during-reading strategies such as visualizing, making intertextual and personal connections, inferencing, and clarifying. With very young children, it is effective to use a sequence of visualization activities based on suggestions by Fredericks (1986). To help children "make pictures in their heads," he suggests starting by holding up concrete objects in class, asking them to close their eyes and "see" the object in their minds. After practice with classroom objects, children can close their eyes and see familiar things such as their bedroom, their mother's face, or their street. After this practice, Fredericks suggests reading aloud to

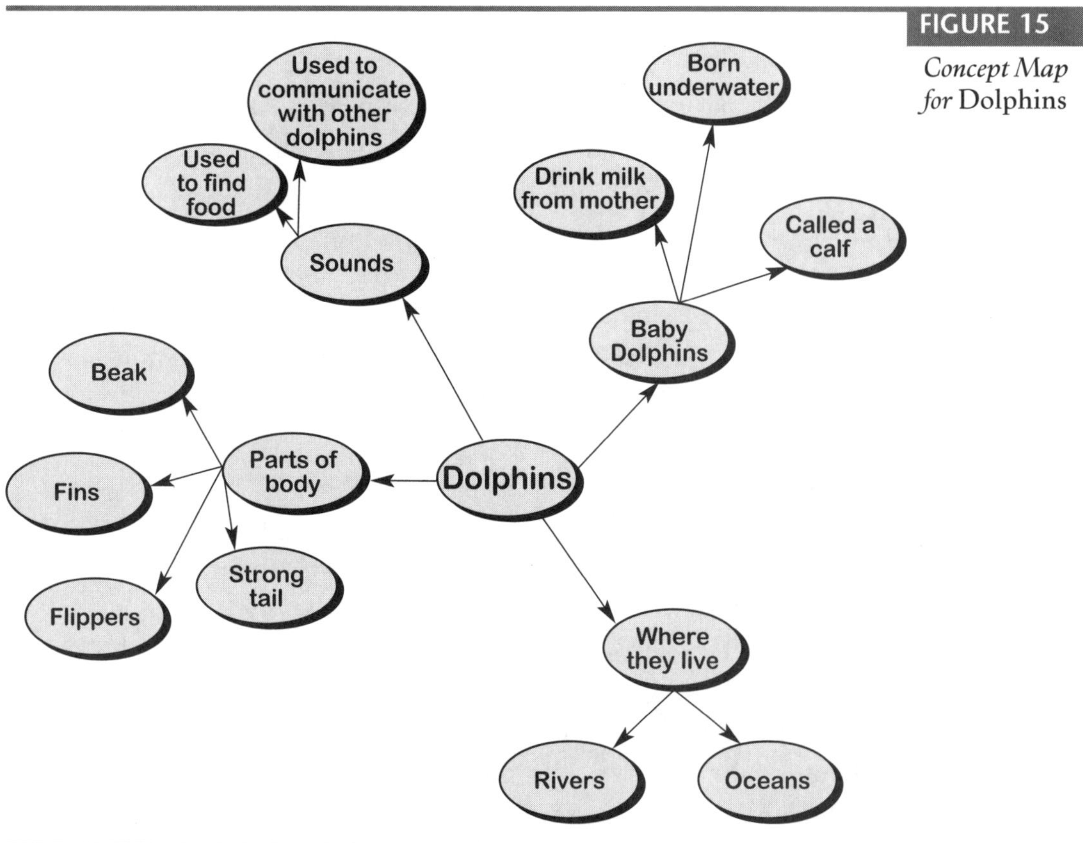

FIGURE 15
Concept Map for Dolphins

them a description of something familiar, such as a dog, and asking them to visualize it. The children can change the pictures in their minds to match the dog's color, size, stance, and activity. This progression helps young children understand what it is to make a picture in their heads. Once children understand the concept, they can visualize using simple informational texts with the illustrations covered so that they use the text rather than the pictures for visual details. A logical extension of visualization is drawing. Children can draw a picture that they see in their minds after they have read or heard informational text. For example, while reading or listening to *If You Hopped Like a Frog* (Schwartz, 1999), children might picture themselves performing some of the amazing feats described and draw what they have pictured as a culminating activity for the lesson.

In order to make inferences, children connect what they already know with what they read (or hear) in the text. This means that it is difficult to make inferences about something they know nothing about. Lessons can be developed in which children are encouraged to "read beyond the text" to make inferences. For example, Cathy Yost's second graders read "As soon as they are born, the pups go their own way. It is not safe to stay near a hungry mother" from *Hungry, Hungry Sharks* (Cole, 1986, p. 24). Cathy asked the children to think about what that might mean: Why would it not be safe to stay near a hungry mother? The children quickly made the inference that mother sharks sometimes eat their babies.

Making connections with what they already know is another strategy that young children can use when reading informational text. Children can learn to make intertextual connections as well as connections with what they have experienced themselves (Oyler, 1996). Use of text sets when exploring particular topics contributes to children's ability and interest in making intertextual connections. Having a list of books that have been used as read-alouds (as suggested in chapter 4) or a list of books that the children have read independently (as suggested in chapter 8) will help them make these intertextual connections.

Clarifying (Palincsar & Brown, 1989) is a strategy that is closely aligned with comprehension monitoring. When children realize that there is something that they do not understand, they should seek to clarify meaning. Sometimes it is a vocabulary word that they do not know; sometimes the difficulty is related to sentence construction or lack of information. It is important that children learn that reading is supposed to make sense, and if it does not, they should go back to the text and try to figure out the answer.

Repeated modeling and discussion of these strategies can encourage children to use strategies when reading independently. Even first graders can talk about intertextual connections, inferencing, clarifying, and making pictures in their heads, becoming metacognitively aware of these strategies when teachers and peers discuss them.

After-Reading Strategies

After reading, teachers want students to reflect on what they have read, integrate new knowledge with what they already know, think about how the reading might be related to their own lives, and be able to apply new knowledge to new situations. Strategies most likely to be useful after reading include creating pictures or graphs and summarizing the material. The kind of reflection necessary to summarize, either in language or in pictures and graphs, helps children check their reading comprehension. Through the deep processing required to convert text into a graphical representation, children strengthen their understanding and also remember the information for a longer time.

Creating Pictures and Graphs

Using pictures or graphs to show understanding seems to be natural for young children. Pictures and graphs tend to come more easily to most children than writing in complete sentences. Indeed, most children draw information before they begin writing it. This natural tendency toward pictures and graphs can be used to help children reflect on information that they have learned from reading independently or listening to a read-aloud. These representations can include concept maps, diagrams, pictures with captions, cause-effect graphics, compare-contrast charts, or timelines.

For example, children who have read *Snake* (Hoffman, 1986) might respond to the information by drawing pictures of the most important ideas, which might include snakes with fangs, snakes shedding their skins, or snakes swallowing their prey. Children could write captions to explain their drawings.

Many teachers use concept mapping in writing instruction to help children think about what they want to write. The same kind of map can be used to help children reflect on information that they have learned from reading *Snake* (see Figure 16). Children's maps could include what snakes eat, what they look like, which ones are poisonous, and who their enemies are.

A more advanced use of graphical representation might be for children who have read Kroll's (1994) account of the Lewis and Clark expedition to create timelines with the important events from the journey

FIGURE 16

Concept Map for Snake

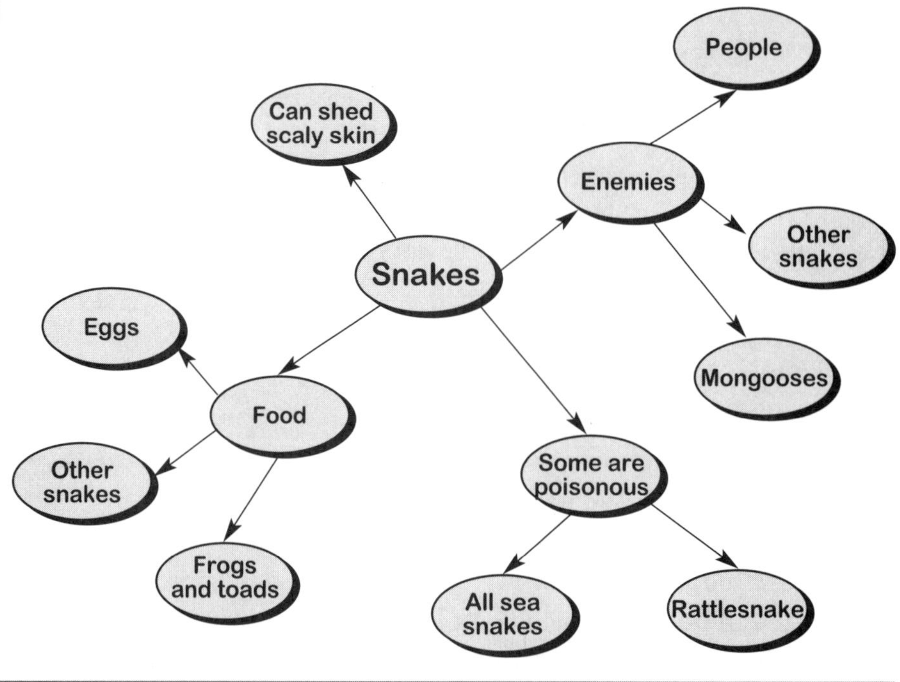

or create maps showing the route that Lewis and Clark took. Also, children might draw pictures of particularly important events during the expedition and provide captions with explanatory information.

Heather McGinn, a teacher in Pennsylvania, encourages her first-grade students to draw pictures to help them think about what they have read or heard. These after-reading products are usually a combination of pictures and text (see Figure 17 for a student's response to reading about alligators). This activity enables students to process the information they have learned.

Summarizing

Summarizing is not an easy strategy, so it is better for students to begin with texts that are short and fairly easy to summarize, such as a magazine article, an Internet source, or part of a book. It is necessary to provide a lot of guidance and practice before expecting children to be able to do this on their own.

A teacher can explain that a summary is a short way of retelling a passage in your own words. Then, she can provide practice with short paragraphs in either small groups or with the whole class. A teacher can encourage children to use their own words to summarize as they discuss text. For example, in *Ruth Law Thrills a Nation* (Brown, 1993), the text states, "She put on two woolen suits, one on top of the other. Then she put on two leather suits and covered her bulky outfit with a skirt" (n.p.). Children can learn to summarize this by stating, "She wore lots of clothes."

Sharon Craig, a former primary-grade teacher in Maryland, has developed a technique that teaches students to summarize. After looking at a text, she and her students generate a question or turn a subheading into a question. Together they read the first sentence, and she asks, "Does this sentence help us answer our question?" If not, they move on to the next sentence. If it does, she says, "Show me the words or phrases we need to highlight that give us this information." Sharon tells the children to imagine that each word costs $1.00, so they have to be careful not to choose too many. They negotiate the words that should be highlighted and then reread only the highlighted part to see if they understand the information. If they select too little information,

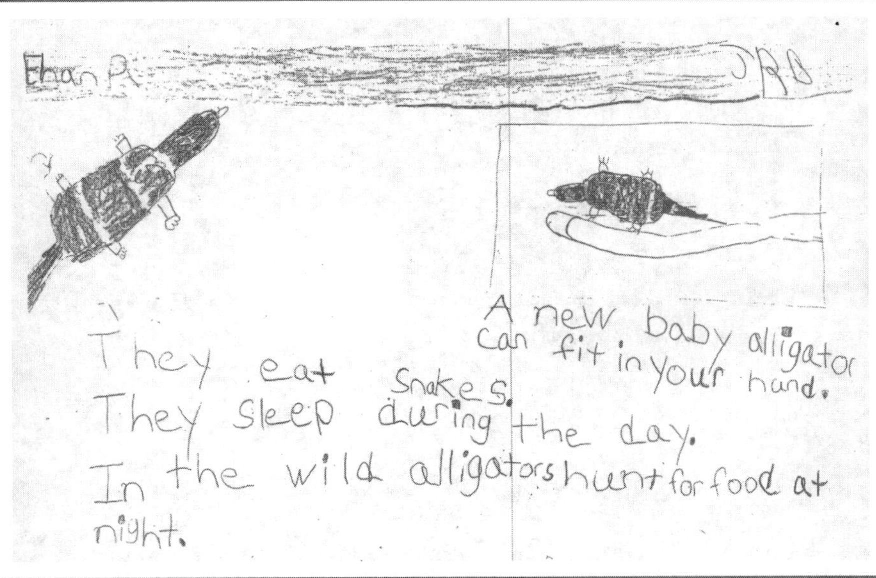

FIGURE 17

Student After-Reading Product

they go back and highlight additional words. They continue in this way until they reach the end of the section, then they reread the question and do a quick read of the highlighted words and phrases to be sure they have answered the question. With first graders and early second graders, Sharon continues to guide the process. With older children, she gradually releases responsibility for the process to them, first through paired work and then through independent practice.

After they have highlighted the information, students construct a concept map using the questions as categories. They copy the highlighted words or phrases under the appropriate categories. They review the maps and check off the most important information. Then they write their summaries using their maps. Through the process, students learn to paraphrase as well as summarize.

Sharon writes, "The process is very concrete, and although time consuming, is very successful. The children not only learn how strategic readers construct and monitor meaning, but they quickly acquire the comprehension strategies for their own use" (personal communication, February, 28, 2003).

Based on the work of Brown, Campione, and Day (1981) and Kintsch and Van Dijk (1978), macro rules for summarizing are as follows:

1. Delete unnecessary material.
2. Delete redundant material.
3. Use one word to replace a list of items.
4. Use one word to replace individual parts of an action.
5. Select or create a topic sentence.

We do not suggest teaching all these rules at one time to primary-grade children; however, they provide a good guide for teachers in planning lessons in summarizing. Children can learn to use these rules as they work with text if they are provided with ample guidance and practice.

Teaching Techniques

As previously explained, the term *strategy* refers to what readers do and *technique* refers to what teachers do. Popular teaching techniques used with informational text often embed the previously discussed comprehension strategies (Bednar & Kletzien, 1993). For example, K-W-L (Ogle, 1986) includes accessing prior knowledge (What I Know), questioning (What I Want to Learn), and summarizing (What I Have Learned). Questioning the Author (Beck, McKeown, Sandora, & Worthy, 1996) uses clarifying, summarizing, and questioning. Reciprocal teaching (Brown & Palincsar, 1985) uses clarifying, questioning, summarizing, and predicting. When we use these teaching techniques with children, we always explain the comprehension strategies that are being used. The goal is for children to learn to use the strategies independently while they are reading. We believe that explicit explanation and practice in connected reading are the best ways for children to become strategic readers.

Orchestrating Several Strategies

Good readers use more than one strategy when they read; they orchestrate several strategies to construct meaning, shifting from one to another and integrating the strategies with ease. The goal is to help children learn to be strategic in their reading by using a repertoire of comprehension strategies.

Susan Smith, a special education teacher in Pennsylvania, showed her group of learning support students how to coordinate questioning, predicting, and making connections as they read *Rosie: A Visiting Dog's Story* (Calmenson, 2001). As Susan worked with this group, it was clear that they had had much experience with informational books. She asked them to look at the pictures and tell what kind of book it is. All the children were able to identify the book as informational because of the photographs. She asked them to think about questions that they might have based on the pictures, and she modeled for them one of her own questions. Each child contributed at least one question based on the pictures, which Susan wrote on the dry-erase board.

One boy predicted that Rosie is a therapy dog. Susan asked him to tell the group what a therapy dog is and why he thought that is what the book is about. After he shared his thoughts, Susan complimented him for making the personal connection and reminded the group to always look for connections to themselves or to other books they have read.

As the children read the book, Susan demonstrated how additional questions are generated based on the text and pictures. One girl commented that she didn't think that dogs were allowed in hospitals, so she wondered why there is a picture of the dog in the hospital.

Susan invited connections between the story and the children's personal experiences with dogs and puppies. When the children's connections began to veer from what was needed to help understand the text, Susan skillfully reminded them that connections are useful only when they further understanding—not when they go off topic.

The group of students was completely engaged with the text. They discussed the issues knowledgeably and were reluctant to put the books away when Susan told them to go to lunch. After checking the answered and remaining questions and with a promise to return to the book the following day, the children left the room still talking about Rosie the visiting dog.

Throughout the lesson, Susan and her students negotiated reading strategically, orchestrating predictions, accessing prior knowledge, making personal connections, and questioning. It is clear that these children with special learning needs were able to use these comprehension strategies effectively.

Summary

Primary-grade children can be taught to use comprehension strategies before, during, and after reading informational text. These strategies can be taught using read-alouds or in small- or large-group instruction. Teachers need to explain the strategies directly, model their use, and provide lots of guided practice. The goal is to help children become strategic readers, able to orchestrate a number of strategies to help themselves comprehend. In the following chapters, we provide suggestions for teaching children to use informational text for research and as models for their own writing.

CHAPTER 6

Using Informational Text and Internet Resources to Teach Search Strategies

As we discussed in chapter 1, primary-grade children in the United States and other countries are now expected to read both fiction and informational text. Further, standardized tests for primary-grade children reflect these demands by including much informational text. But today's young children are expected to do more than simply read and comprehend informational material. They must be able to locate information using a variety of sources, to compare and contrast information across sources, and to integrate information from multiple sources.

These demands are evident in the influential report of the Committee on the Prevention of Reading Difficulties in Young Children (Snow, Burns, & Griffin, 1998). The committee indicates that kindergarten children should "demonstrate familiarity with a number of types or genres of text (e.g., storybooks, expository texts, poems, newspapers, and everyday print)" (p. 80) and that first through third graders should be able to read grade-appropriate fiction and informational text. In addition, second graders should be able to "read nonfiction materials for answers to specific questions or for specific purposes" and should "connect and compare information across nonfiction selections" (p. 82). Third graders should be able to combine "information from multiple sources in writing reports" (p. 83), and by the time they complete third grade, they must be "capable—independently and productively—of reading to learn" (p. 207).

To be capable of independently reading to learn, young children must be information literate. As the American Association of School Librarians (AASL; 1998) argues, information literacy underlies the development of independent learners. In its information literacy standards, the AASL states that an information-literate student "accesses information efficiently and effectively," "evaluates information critically and competently," and "uses information accurately and creatively" (n.p.). If students are to become information literate, then teachers must begin developing these abilities in the early grades. This chapter will explore how to help young children learn to use informational books and Internet resources so that they can find the information they need and want.

Teaching Children to Use Book Features to Search for Information

Even in kindergarten, children are expected to know "the parts of a book and their function" (Snow et al., 1998, p. 80). But as more informational books are introduced in the early grades, book features proliferate and children need to be acquainted with them.

Many features of informational books are useful to children as they seek answers to their questions. Common features include tables of contents, headings and subheadings, and glossaries and indexes (see Figure 18). Many books also have maps, diagrams, illustrations, captions, and boldface for specialized terms. Sometimes there are brief

FIGURE 18

Common Features of Informational Books

Table of contents
Glossary
Index
Headings and subheadings
Maps
Diagrams
Illustrations
Captions
Boldface type for specialized terms
Cover information (e.g., descriptions of content or purpose-setting questions)
Author's note
Supplements to the main text
Acknowledgments to experts, consultants
Suggestions for further reading

descriptions of the content or purpose-setting questions on the front or back covers that may help children decide if a book is likely to contain information they are seeking. In addition, authors may include notes on sources, acknowledgments to experts, and supplemental information that extends the content.

To introduce children to book features, teachers can use the very effective technique—read-alouds (see chapter 4). For example, in a unit on penguins, a teacher read a selection of books about the topic, each with different search features. One book, *The Emperor's Egg* (Jenkins, 1999), provides many facts while telling the story of a male emperor penguin who hatches the egg his mate has laid. Because *The Emperor's Egg* is a narrative-informational book, the teacher read it from start to finish. As they discussed this book, the children wanted to know more about penguins. They posed many questions, and the teacher brought to class other books about penguins that might offer answers. Sharing these books during read-alouds allowed her to explain and model the search features.

One of the books, *Penguins* (Robinson, 1997), an expository-informational book, contained a table of contents, index, glossary, boldface type for terms, and a list of more books to read on the topic. The teacher began by having children recall the questions they had after listening to *The Emperor's Egg*. For example, several children wanted to know more about penguins' eggs and babies. The teacher pointed out that there is often more than one way to find out if a book has the information they need. Using *Penguins*, she first showed them the table of contents and explained what it does. Then she read the contents page, and the children noted that there were sections on eggs, babies, and growing up. They decided to start with these sections. Later, the teacher showed the children how to check the index for information to answer their other questions. She was able to show her students that not all informational books need to be read from start to finish. She also was able to demonstrate that it may be necessary to read only part of a book when looking for specific information.

The teacher also helped her students compare the search features of other books on penguins, noting that some have many features while others have none. The children talked about the books that might best serve specific purposes. As they explored the books, the children went well beyond tables of contents and indexes. For example, they learned why some words are highlighted in boldface. The teacher pointed out a note at the bottom of the copyright page in *Penguins*: "Some words are shown in bold, **like this**. You can find out what they mean by looking in the glossary." Together the teacher and children located a word in bold and then checked out its meaning in the glossary at the back of the book.

Read-alouds are also good vehicles for modeling the conventions that will help children to use search features effectively. For example, children need to know how alphabetical order works in indexes. Information on Harriet Tubman will be under *T* not *H* in the index of *Life on the Underground Railroad* (Isaacs, 2002). Children need to know the difference between index entries of page numbers that read "3–6" versus "3, 6." Further, they need to know how to think of different terms if the ones they are looking for are not there. This may lead to talking about synonyms or terms that subsume the word they are looking for; for instance, they may need to look up *games* or *toys* if *fun* is not listed.

Helping Children Transfer What They Learn

We know from research that even older students have trouble with search skills because they fail to transfer out-of-context lessons to independent learning (Dreher & Sammons, 1994). Thus, we recommend modeling the use of search features and their conventions in meaningful contexts for real purposes. Doing so helps ensure that children will actually transfer the instruction to other contexts.

The case of one young boy illustrates this point. After experiencing his teacher explaining and modeling the use of tables of contents and indexes during read-alouds, the boy showed that he clearly understood that these features allow a directed search. He wanted specific information on the size and weight of whales. He found a book on whales but noted that it had no index or table of contents. His options would be to read, skim, or scan the entire book; but with no headings, boldface, or other helpful features, it would be a daunting task. He quickly proclaimed, "I'd have to read the whole thing!" and decided to try another book.

For some purposes, reading the entire book is fine; but for seeking information about specific questions, it would not be very efficient. Therefore, it is important to teach children about search features and how to select books for different purposes so that they can make informed decisions when they seek information. When search features are modeled in meaningful contexts, children do learn their uses and value.

Helping Children Note Variations of Informational Book Features

As children seek answers, they will find that not all indexes are alike—indexes differ in format and complexity. Similarly, other features of informational books vary as well. Teachers can help children become more effective searchers by pointing out the variations in particular features across books. The following examples illustrate the variety of features that children may encounter.

In many books, the table of contents is quite simple. *Trees* (Lessor, 2004) lists 3 sections and a glossary. Other tables of contents are lengthier. The contents for *Reptiles* (Meadows & Vail, 2002) lists 10 sections plus a glossary and index, even though the book is the same length as *Trees*. Some tables of contents have more complex formats. In *Platypus* (Short, Green, & Bird, 1997), the table of contents is arranged in two columns with subheadings under each main heading (see Figure 19).

Indexes also vary. Some are on one page in one column, as in *Platypus* (Short et al., 1997), while others may be on one page but in three columns, as in *Thieves & Rascals* (Balance, 2002). Still other indexes continue beyond one page; for example, *The Kingfisher First Animal Encyclopedia* (Farndon & Kirkwood, 1998) has a multiple-page, triple-column index. There are also picture indexes in which a picture is accompanied by a page number or in which both a picture and a word appear with a page number, as in *Animal Legs* (Theodorou, 1998). Still other books have a feature not labeled as an index but that is similar. For example, *Soaring Bald Eagles* (Martin-James, 2001) closes with a page titled "Hunt and Find" with an entries such as "an eagle **diving** on page 12." The book *Big Machines* (Wallace, 2000) has a

FIGURE 19

A Complex Contents Page

Contents

From Platypus. *Short, J., Green, J., & Bird, B. (1997). Ill. A. Wichlinski. New York: Mondo.*

"Picture Word List" that is a combination of a glossary and an index (e.g., the word *shovel*, accompanied by a photograph and page number).

There also is a great deal of variation in captions and labels for illustrations. Because children can learn much from illustrations in informational books, they need to be aware of the differences. The captions in *A Primary Source Guide to China* (Roza, 2003) have directional triangles that point toward the appropriate illustrations. In *Amazing Snakes* (Parsons, 1990), many illustrations have captions with arrows that point to a specific place in the illustration being discussed, as when an arrow links the sentence "The egg-eating snake can swallow a bird's egg twice the size of its head" (p. 15) to an illustration of a hugely expanded section of a snake's body. But in other cases, information about illustrations is found in the back of the book. For example, the last page of *Thinking About Ants* (Brenner, 1997) identifies the type of ants shown in each illustration: "Pages 2–3: Black carpenter ants on cherry tree." In *About Mammals: A Guide for Children* (Sill, 1997), each painting of a mammal is labeled in the text (e.g., "Plate 15 Arctic Fox"); but for details, readers must consult the afterword where small black-and-white reproductions of the paintings are accompanied by more information (e.g., "Plate 15 The white winter coats of Arctic Foxes change to brown in summer. This camouflage or protective coloration allows them to hide from both predators and prey" (n.p.).

Children also need to know that different terms may be used for features in informational books. Most of the tables of contents we have seen are simply labeled *Contents*. However, in some books children may encounter other labels. In *Bears* (Kalman & Everts, 1994), the contents page is labeled "What is in this book?" Similarly, glossaries are sometimes called something else. In *Bears*, the glossary is labeled "Words to know." In *Life in a Pond* (Fowler, 1996), a picture glossary titled "Words You Know" contains photos with words such as *lake* and *marsh* appearing under the appropriate photos.

Although at first glance all this variation may seem overwhelming for primary-grade students, it really is not. Children can handle variation if they are given the opportunity. They learn as their teachers model how to use various formats of contents pages and other features. With lots of opportunity to experience informational books in read-alouds and strategy instruction across the content areas, children develop flexibility.

To encourage flexibility, teachers can show children how to preview a book to find out what features are available. A quick look at the front and back pages will reveal much about how information can be accessed. A preview of *Soaring Bald Eagles* (Martin-James, 2001) shows that it has no table of contents, but in the back it has a map to show where eagles live, a diagram of an eagle's body parts, a glossary, an index-like feature, an acknowledgment, and a section about the author. Children can also look for notes that explain a book's features, such as a note about the use of boldface type to flag glossary words. Reference volumes for young children often include explanations. Just before the main text begins in *The Kingfisher First Animal Encyclopedia* (Farndon & Kirkwood, 1998), there are examples of each type of illustration and other conventions used in the book (see Figure 20).

FIGURE 20

Explanation of Book's Conventions

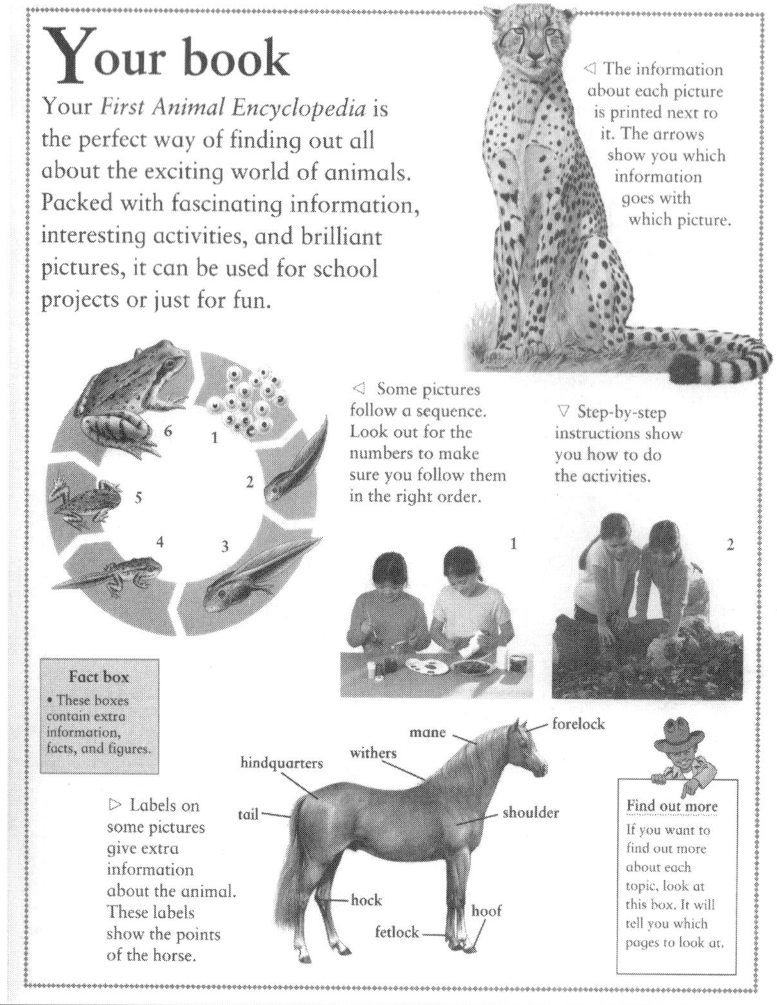

From The Kingfisher First Animal Encyclopedia. *Farndon, J., & Kirkwood, J. (1998). Reprinted with permission of Kingfisher Publications.*

Helping Children Monitor Information Searches

As teachers model searching for information, children will want to try it too. Just as we indicated for strategy instruction (see chapter 5), teachers should gradually release the responsibility for locating information to the children. After having opportunities to pose questions and find information with their teacher, children can work in pairs or small groups before trying individual tasks.

One way teachers can assist children as they move toward seeking answers on their own is to talk with them about what they have noticed about how to find information as their teachers have modeled the search process. Studies of how people locate information for specific purposes indicate that efficient searchers typically (a) formulate a goal, (b) select appropriate categories of a text to examine, (c) extract relevant information, (d) integrate extracted information with what they already know, and (e) monitor whether more information is needed (Dreher, 2002). If children see their teacher modeling the search for information, they will notice many of these processes. Young children need not learn a formal model, nor do they need to learn these particular terms. But as they discuss how to find information, they will likely come up with similar concepts.

As teachers and students talk about what is involved in a search for information, they may want to develop a list of questions to help guide the search process. These questions are likely to parallel the steps they have seen modeled and will, of course, parallel the processes that have been identified in research. The following questions (adapted from Dreher, 1992) may emerge as children discuss searching for information.

Before starting to search for information, children need to formulate a goal. An appropriate reminder question might be **What information do I need?**

Once children are clear about what they are searching for, they need to decide which features in a book, or other resource, might offer the best route to the information. An appropriate question for this step might be **Does this book (website or magazine) have search features that would help me find what I want to know?**

After children have located a portion of text to inspect, they must extract relevant information. Questions to guide this process include **Is the information I need located here? Does the information I have located make sense?** At this point, children also should think about accuracy with a question such as **Is there anything in this book (or website or magazine) to help me decide whether the information is correct?**

Once children have located information they judge to be relevant, they need to integrate it with prior knowledge or with other information they have already located. They might ask **Does this information relate to things I already know?**

Children also need to monitor the completeness of the answer so that they can go back for more information if necessary. An appropriate question might be **Do I have all the information that I need to answer my question? If not, I should continue searching.**

Questions such as these could be posted in the classroom to use as a guide or checklist when children are looking for information (see Appendix C, page 133).

Searching Internet Resources

In today's information age, even young children need to know how to seek answers to their questions using Internet resources. Not only does the Internet offer all sorts of information to complement books and other material, children find the Internet very motivating, as we noted in chapter 2.

A useful way to guide children to appropriate websites and to help make their use of the Internet more efficient is to select websites ahead of time and organize them into webpages. There are many good search engines and directories that teachers can use to identify appropriate sites for children (see chapter 2). Once teachers have identified websites on a particular topic, they can use a webpage program to organize them in an attractive display. It has been our experience that teachers find webpages easy to create using webpage programs that can be found in word-processing software such as Microsoft Word.

Although we use the term *webpage*, the webpages that teachers create do not necessarily have to be posted on the Internet. They may be housed on a disk and used as needed. When teachers want their students to use these links, they can insert the disk.

If teachers choose to post their webpages on the Internet, then children and their parents can access them from home as well as at school. Teachers may find that their school system offers a website on which they can post their webpages, or they can use one of the many websites that provide templates and assistance to help teachers create and post webpages. Teacherweb (http://teacherweb.com), which charges a modest fee, is an example of such a website specifically aimed at teachers.

Teachers also can use free services like Backflip (www.backflip.com/login.ihtml), a site on which users can select and organize websites. Renee Miller and Sandy Greim Connor, primary-grade teachers in Pennsylvania, use Backflip to show children (and parents) which sites are good for the research projects they are doing. Renee and Sandy have set up Backflip websites with separate folders for each of the research activities that their students are working on. Their students go to the Backflip website, log in using their class's account, select the folder for the topic they are researching, and then go to any of the websites listed. For example, Sandy has set up a Solar System folder with links to NASA (http://pds.jpl.nasa.gov/planets/welcome.htm), NASA Kids (www.kidsastronomy.com), Astronomy for Kids (www.frontiernet.net/~kidpower/astronomy.html), and Zoom Astronomy (www.zoomastronomy.com).

Many other primary-grade teachers also find the Internet to be a wonderful source of information for their students. Helena Akeefe, a second-grade teacher in Maryland, created a webpage to supplement other materials for a unit on butterflies. One of her links is to a website with butterfly photographs (www.butterflywebsite.com/gallery/index.cfm). Helena notes that "Usually our students get so interested in the type of butterflies that we keep in the room that they think those are the only ones that exist. This link will let students see that there are many different types of butterflies with different names and from different parts of the world" (personal communication, May 8, 2003). Another link is to a comprehensive website that gives information on butterflies state by state, as well as offering advice on establishing butterfly gardens and butterfly-related arts and crafts (www.butterflies.com). In addition, Helena includes links to Chicago's Field Museum (www.fmnh.org/butterfly) and to the American Museum of Natural History, which includes (www.amnh.org/exhibitions/butterflies/tour.html) a virtual tour of a butterfly conservatory and live Web cams and video clips of butterflies (www.amnh.org/exhibitions/butterflies/cams.html). Links such as these, along with books, magazines, and hands-on projects, offer students multiple ways of gathering information on a topic.

Michelle Koopman, a first-grade teacher in Maryland, created a webpage with links to websites of authors commonly read in first grade such as Jan Brett, Eric Carle, Mem Fox, Robert Munsch, Dav Pilkey, Dr. Seuss, and Audrey Wood. For example, the site for Dav Pilkey (author of the Captain Underpants series) contains information about his life, factors that influenced his writing, how to contact him, and his policy on speaking to school groups (www.pilkey.com/index.php).

To create her webpage, Michelle involved her students. The students worked in teams to become experts on particular authors by reading about them on author websites. The students also sent e-mails to ask for more information. Each team then wrote short, persuasive texts to convince readers to select their author's website (see chapter 7 for more on persuasive writing). Michelle included the children's comments next to each link on the webpage. As Michelle observed, "Using the Internet to find answers to questions that students have about an author is a valuable lesson about real reading for a purpose" (personal communication, May 8, 2003).

Evaluating Information

When children find information, they need to evaluate it. Part of evaluation involves children deciding whether the information makes sense based on what they set out to find. If children are clear about what information they are searching for, it will be easier to know if they have found it. This may sound obvious, but the first information that catches a child's eye may not be the information that is needed. For example, Dreher (1992) found that when older students were looking for answers to questions, some simply turned to the page indicated in the index and selected the boldface terms they found there, even though the terms did not answer the question.

Problems like these can be reduced when information seeking occurs in meaningful contexts for real purposes, as we have noted. In addition, children can learn to evaluate information by asking themselves questions such as What information do I need? and Does the information I have located make sense? (See Appendix C, page 133.)

Another aspect of evaluating information is to decide whether the information is accurate. Teachers can help children learn to apply many of the same standards they themselves use to evaluate accuracy when choosing books for their classrooms (see chapter 3). For example, teachers can lead children to notice if authors are experts on the topic they are writing about or if they have consulted those who are. Teachers also can help children to notice copyright dates in an effort to assess currency. In addition, teachers can model their own thinking, letting children know that these are not guarantees but that they do provide some information. Children can learn to look for features that relate to accurate content by asking themselves questions about whether there is anything in the book (or website or magazine) to help decide whether the information is correct (see Appendix C, page 133).

Children also can learn to assess accuracy by consulting more than one source. By comparing answers across books and websites, they learn about differences of opinion as well as differences in depth of coverage.

Whether using books or websites, children can learn to evaluate information in much the same way. Just as with a book, teachers can introduce and model how to evaluate a website. As teachers check the date a website was last updated, locate the sponsoring agency, and evaluate contributor qualifications, children learn what to look for. Children can gradually begin to evaluate sites, working first with peers and then individually.

Taking Notes and Organizing Information

Whether children gather information from books or Internet sources, they often need to record information for later use. The information may be needed to refer to in discussions, for creating projects, or for writing (see chapter 7). If children learn to take notes and organize the information they find, it will be much easier for them to use the information later. There are many ways to help young children learn to take notes and organize information. For example, children can use sticky notes, databases, and I-charts.

Using Sticky Notes

Just as sticky notes are good for recording and categorizing questions (see chapter 5), they are also useful for organizing the information children find. As teachers model finding information, they can show children how to record the information on sticky notes. Later, sticky notes can be moved around to group related information. Index cards or sheets of paper can serve the same purpose—they can be sorted and taped onto a blackboard, tag board, or chart paper.

Using Databases

Databases are another appealing way to organize notes and information. Databases are computer software programs in which information is entered into specific user-determined fields; they allow teachers and students to collect specific kinds of information and organize it in many different ways. For example, if a class is interested in finding out about animals that live in the ocean, a teacher can create fields in a database for topics that the teacher and students decide are important. These fields might include *classification*, *size*, *color*, *enemies*, *food*, and *habitat*. Then, as students research various ocean creatures, they can enter the data into the appropriate fields. For example, one group of children might choose to research seahorses. The book *Seahorses* (James, 2002) would inform them that seahorses are fish, and the children would enter that fact in the *classification* database field. They would also discover that seahorses are 1.5 to 12 inches long, live only in warm shallow seawater, and can change color. The children would enter this information in the appropriate database fields. It is important that enough space be left in the fields for a brief identification of the source used; for example, the *classification* entry might read "fish, James, 2002."

It is crucial for the teacher to provide structure for using a database. Children must spell terms correctly because computers do not recognize variations on spelling. In addition, the teacher and students need to specify exactly which words will be used in the database, and to use those words consistently, because computers do not recognize such terms as *shallow* and *not deep* as equivalent. To help avoid such problems, teachers can set up a database with word choices built into a pull-down menu. For example, for the *classification* field, teachers could build in the choices *fish*, *mammal*, and *crustacean*. When children want to add the classification for an ocean animal, they can simply click on the appropriate word rather than typing it.

Once the database is complete, children can sort the information according to any of the included fields. For example, they could create a book based on habitat (animals who live in shallow water; animals who live in deep water) or one based on classification (fish, mammals, crustaceans). For each page of the book, children could create an illustration of the animal and explain what they have learned about that animal (see chapter 7 for more ideas on writing).

Using I-Charts

I-charts also are useful for taking notes and organizing information. I-charts are simply grids that can be formatted as needed (Hoffman, 1992). For example, after reading or listening to *Dogs* (Miller, 1998) and *Cats* (Miller, 1998) for a unit on pets, children might seek information on other pets. As they search in books and other resources, they can record what they find on an I-chart (see Figure 21), adding more pets and questions as desired.

Some books for young children include examples of I-charts that show ways of organizing and summarizing information. Books in the Animal Babies series, such as *Mammals* (Theodorou, 2000), include a table that compares all the animals in the series (see Figure 22). This table lets children easily see which animals are alike or different on key characteristics. Children can make similar tables on other topics.

As children learn to gather information, they also need to learn to credit their sources. An I-chart can be easily adapted for this purpose

FIGURE 21

I-Chart for Pets

	Dogs	Cats	Goldfish	Hamsters	Rabbits	Gerbils
How to tell if they are healthy						
How to feed them						
How to keep them clean						

FIGURE 22

I-Chart Comparing Animal Characteristics

Mammals and Other Animals

		Fish	Amphibians	Insects	Reptiles	Birds	Mammals
What they look like:	Bones inside body	all	all	none	all	all	all
	Number of legs	none	4 or none	6	4 or none	2	2 or 4
	Hair on body	none	none	all	none	none	all
	Scaly skin	most	none	none	all	none	few
	Wings	none	none	most	none	all	some
	Feathers	none	none	none	none	all	none
Where they live:	Live on land	none	most	most	most	all	most
	Live in water	all	some	some	some	none	some
How they are born:	Grow babies inside body	some	few	some	some	none	most
	Hatch from eggs	most	most	most	most	all	few
How babies get food:	Get milk from mother	none	none	none	none	none	all
	Parents bring food	none	none	none	none	most	most

From Mammals. *Theodorou, R. (2000). Reprinted with permission of Heinemann Library.*

by adding a source column, which allows children to compare the information in different books on the same topic (see Figure 23).

As with other techniques, modeling is an excellent way to introduce I-charts. For example, a teacher led children to investigate how cheetahs and lions are alike and different. She began by posing a specific question about the two animals' hunting practices and guiding children to scan the table of contents of *Cheetah* (Meadows & Vail, 2002). The students found two relevant sections: (1) How They Hunt and (2) What They Hunt. Similarly, the table of contents of *Lions* (Meadows & Vail, 2000) also has two relevant sections: (1) How They Hunt and (2) Their Diet. Working together, the teacher and students concluded that these would be good sections to read. The teacher then read aloud those sections and modeled for students how to take notes to answer the question. After they answered the first question, the teacher and students posed another question and determined whether *Cheetahs* and *Lions* had relevant information. Figure 24 shows an example of how the teacher modeled the rephrasing of text information, which results in notes containing complete sentences. However, in other cases, teachers will want to show children how to use key words and phrases in their note-taking (see chapter 5).

Once children understand how to use an I-chart, they can use it on their own and modify it for their own purposes. In addition, children can use other types of graphic organizers, such as those discussed in chapter 5, to take and organize notes. Children also can use these charts to help guide their writing (see chapter 7).

FIGURE 23

I-Chart Using Two Sources on Deserts

	Questions		
Sources	1. What is a desert?	2. Where are the world's deserts?	3. What animals live in the desert?
Deserts (Wilkes, 1990)			
Deserts (Morris, 1996)			

FIGURE 24

I-Chart Comparing Lions and Cheetahs

Sources	Questions	
	1. What do they hunt? How do they hunt it?	2. What are their families like?
Lions (Meadow & Vail, 2000)	They look for sick or old animals because they are easier to catch. They eat both big and small animals. Females do most of the hunting. Lion cubs start hunting when they are 2 years old. When they hunt, they catch the animal about one out of four tries.	
Cheetahs (Meadows & Vail, 2000)	They look for old or hurt animals that are slow. They eat small animals like rabbits, birds, antelopes. They also eat the babies of larger animals like zebras. They hide in tall grass and sneak up as close as they can. Then they chase the animal. Chases are very short, less than a minute. They don't hunt in the middle of the day when it is hot. When they hunt, they catch the animal about half the time.	

Summary

Today's children are expected be information literate. They need to know how to find information in books as well as on the Internet. Teachers can help children develop information literacy by providing many opportunities for children to seek information in meaningful contexts for real purposes. With informational books and websites, teachers can model how to use search features, how to monitor the search for information, how to evaluate found information, and how to take notes and organize information. Chapter 7 shows teachers how to help young children use the information they have found to write informational text.

CHAPTER 7

Teaching Children to Write Informational Text

Just as most of the reading we do as adults is informational text, most of the writing we do is also informational. Yet in a recent report, the National Commission on Writing in America's Schools and Colleges (2003) concluded that writing is the "neglected 'R.'" The report quotes U.S. Bureau of Labor Statistics data that indicate that "More than 90 percent of midcareer professionals recently cited the 'need to write effectively' as a skill 'of great importance' in their day-to-day work" (p. 11).

The National Assessment of Educational Progress measures children's ability to write narrative, informative, and persuasive texts at grades 4, 8, and 12 (Greenwald, Persky, Campbell, & Mazzeo, 2002). Because children are expected to be able to write all three types of texts by fourth grade, it is important that teachers introduce children to all types in the primary grades.

"When children are given the opportunity and encouragement, they will write texts with structures that are similar to the texts they read—stories, rhymes and informational texts" (Hiebert & Raphael, 1998, p. 149). Because reading and writing develop together, writing informational texts can be a natural outgrowth of the reading that primary teachers encourage in their classrooms. If teachers have used informational books for read-alouds and in reading instruction, as suggested in previous chapters, children should be familiar with these forms.

Informational writing involves children in expressing their interest and knowledge about the world around them. They can write several kinds of informational texts for different purposes and for different audiences. They can write from personal knowledge and experience, and they can research topics to become experts and write about what they have learned. In fact, "writing is a powerful means of organizing thinking, or making sense of experience" (Mallett, 1999, p. 107).

One of the ways that teachers can use informational writing is to ask children to do a "quick write" about what they have learned about a particular topic, either from a read-aloud or from reading and discussing texts. This kind of writing is informal and is used to help students clarify and organize what they have learned. It is a good place to begin asking young children to write from sources rather than from their own experiences.

Cathy Yost, a second-grade teacher in Pennsylvania, often uses this kind of writing with her students. She invites them to listen to a read-aloud as a whole class, to read and discuss related texts as small groups, and then to write individually what they have learned about the topic in their writing journals (see Figure 25 for a student journal entry on sharks). She asks students to write about what they found most interesting, and then the class shares what they have written with one another. As one child reads, the other children check their writing to see whether they have included the same information.

More formal writing assignments also are appropriate in the primary grades. These assignments should include lots of prewriting

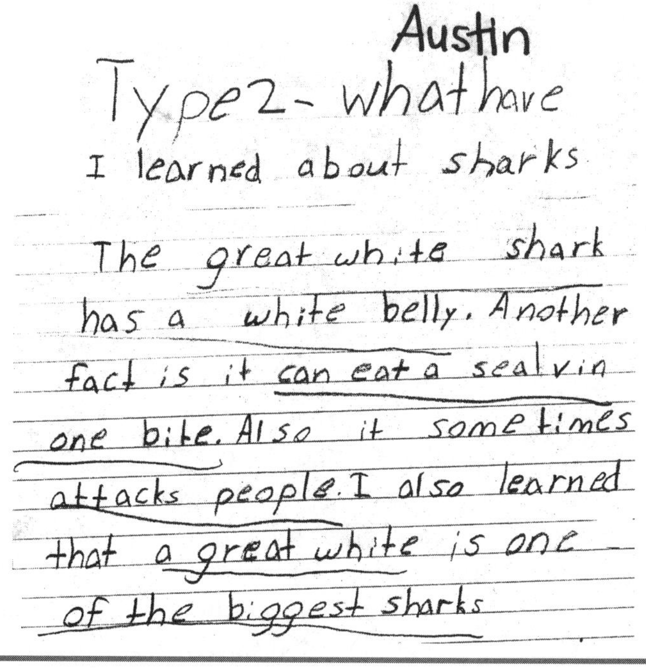

Austin

Type2- what have I learned about sharks

The great white shark has a white belly. Another fact is it can eat a seal in one bite. Also it sometimes attacks people. I also learned that a great white is one of the biggest sharks

FIGURE 25

Example of Student Writing Journal

discussions and activities and time for drafting, revising, editing, and, finally, sharing with others. Children should be urged to always think of their audience while writing.

Whenever children are expected to write in a particular form, they need to be provided with many examples to explore. For example, if children are asked to write procedural text, teachers can read several procedural texts along with them, inviting them to notice how the authors have written the text and having them identify particular characteristics of those texts. As Stead (2002) states, "If we truly want to extend children's understanding of various nonfictional writing forms, we need to lead them to discover what it is that writers do when they write to inform...their readers" (p. 145).

Types of Informational Writing

Wray and Lewis (1997) identify several types of informational writing that primary-grade children can use: recount, report, procedure, explanation, and argument (persuasion). Each type has a different purpose and particular characteristics (see Appendix A, page 126). We explain how a teacher might help children learn to write in each of these forms.

Recounts

A recount is simply a retelling of an event or experience. This is perhaps the easiest type of informational text that young children can write. Children usually have had a lot of practice in creating oral recounts because they are often called on to describe what happened at a particular event or time. Knowing that these can be written is the basis for learning to write a recount.

Children often are asked to recount their experiences as shared writing with the teacher or in writing workshop or as daily journals. The purpose of a recount is to relate an experience to the reader. It is usually written in past tense and in sequential order.

When talking to young children about how to write recounts, teachers can demonstrate how this is done through shared writing. One teacher modeled this through a recount of a field trip that the children had taken. She set the purpose for the recount with the statement "On Monday, our class visited the courthouse."

Then, she modeled writing each of the important things that the class saw or learned in sequence. She asked for suggestions from the class as the recount developed. She used past tense, which is typical of recounts, and concluded with the statement "We had a good time at the courthouse."

Students will need more than one example to learn the characteristics of recounts. Teachers can offer students additional shared writing recounts to examine or provide texts written as recounts such as memoirs, biographies, and autobiographies. Children should be encouraged to discuss and list the characteristics of recounts, a more effective technique than simply telling them what they are. As students identify the characteristics, the teacher can put them on a chart for students to use later as they write their own recounts. The chart might include the following:

Has a beginning sentence that tells what it is about

Is written in past tense

Includes words such as *then* and *next*

Tells about a real experience

Is written in order

Has an ending sentence

Teachers can help children plan for their recounts by discussing an event, thinking about what they did, and using a sequence map (see chapter 5). Writing recounts usually is easy for children because recounts grow from personal experiences, such as one second grader's recount of a class trip to a pond (see Figure 26).

FIGURE 26

Student Recount of Trip to Pond

My trip to the pond

Hi! My name is Bryan. One day I went to the pond with my class. My school has a pond in our environmental center. At the pond I saw a slimy slug on a big gray rock. I saw small black fish. I saw a big gray squirll as big as a rabbit chewing on a delicous nut. I saw a huge yellow bee's nest with tiny holes in it next to an oak tree. Guess what! I saw a fossil of a shell! I saw tiny black ants as small as peas crawing up a big tree trunk. It was an exiting trip to the pond! I loved it very much! I'd like to come again!

Reports

Reports are the kind of writing most often associated with informational text. The purpose of a report is to describe something—an animal, a state, a plant, a building, or anything that a child would be interested in describing. Unlike recounts, reports are usually written in present tense, indicating the timelessness of the information. They feature factual information and often include pictures with captions or labels and diagrams. Reports often are structured like a description, but they could also reflect other structures such as cause-effect or comparison-contrast (see chapter 5). Often children engage in research in order to be able to write reports, but reports also can include personal experiences.

As with other forms of writing, children need to have experiences reading and discussing reports. After they have had time to examine reports and identify characteristics, they will be ready to begin writing.

Fortunately, there are many excellent books that fall into the category of reports. Books written about animals, people, places, or events are often written in the form of reports. Teachers who use informational books as read-alouds and as part of reading instruction will have children who are familiar with the characteristics of reports.

Teachers and children could review some of these books and student samples from previous years, identifying common characteristics of reports. Teachers can revisit expository-informational books that they have used as read-alouds, encouraging the children to talk about the features. For example, *Arctic Foxes and Red Foxes* (Meadows & Vail, 2002) could be used to talk about the kind of language used, the kinds of facts that the authors have given about the two kinds of foxes, the illustrations related to the text, the comparison-contrast structure, and the headings used.

Children might be particularly interested in looking at *Penguins Are Waterbirds* (Taberski, 2002) because it was written by a first-grade class. Again, it is helpful if the children themselves generate the characteristics. The teacher can put them on a chart to be posted in the room to remind children as they write. Some of the characteristics to be identified include the following:

Has a beginning sentence that draws readers' interest

Is written using present-tense verbs, indicating the timelessness of the information

Includes general statements about the topic rather than specific individuals (i.e., “a fox” or “foxes” instead of “Father Fox”)

Uses factual information

Presents diagrams or pictures with labels and captions

Has an ending sentence

Children should have a choice in what they write about in reports, because they will be more successful when motivated by interest. Children enjoy sharing with others what they have learned about a favorite subject and usually have more prior knowledge about a subject in which they are interested.

One of the biggest concerns for teachers is that children may copy directly from the Internet or an encyclopedia when they are writing reports. Often this is because the reading material that they are using is too difficult for them to understand (Mallett, 1999). It is important that children be able to read at an independent or instructional level when they are doing research for a report. This means, of course, that teachers need to have many resources written at different levels available for their classroom of young researchers.

It is important to have several sources for each possible topic that children will choose. One way to be sure to have enough resources is to limit children’s choices to topics for which there are enough books. Another way to make resources go further is to have children work in groups. Teachers can work with school and public librarians to identify a collection of books, magazines, websites, and articles for the children to use.

As mentioned in chapter 6, many websites, even those created for children, feature text that is difficult for the intended grade level (Kamil & Lane, 1998), so teacher guidance plays an important role in helping children choose sites that they can understand easily. Some teachers have voiced concern that well-meaning parents sometimes help children search for information on the Web for research, but the found information is far too difficult for children to understand. It is a good idea at the beginning of a research project to send a letter home to parents explaining what the children are doing and alerting parents to the problems of giving children text that is too difficult. It is useful also to let children and parents know about particular websites that may be useful in the research (see chapter 6).

If children use graphic organizers, I-charts, or databases, as described in chapters 5 and 6, they will be more likely to use their own words in their reports. Children often take notes on the graphic organizers or I-charts by using only key words, not complete sentences. When children begin to write their reports, the key words help them remember the information, but not the exact wording of the article, book, or website. Thus, they use their own words to rephrase the information in sentences.

Young children need structure to help them organize their research and note-taking before they begin writing. When Kathy Simpson, a second-grade teacher in Pennsylvania, helps students organize their research and report writing, she leads them through a discussion about the kinds of information they are interested in finding. Then she provides them with photocopied sheets of their questions to take notes on (see Appendix C, page 134). She leaves spaces for what they already know about the topic and what they learn through their research.

Kathy teaches her students how to find information in an informational book or on the Internet, how to take notes, how to create an interesting opening for their reports, how to organize their reports into paragraphs that answer the questions they plan to research, how to write a concluding sentence, and how to use their own words in their writing. She uses samples of other students' writing and models how to accomplish these goals. Kathy finds it helpful to provide students with a checklist so they can evaluate their own work (see Appendix C, page 135).

Using effective instruction and modeling, Kathy works with her second-grade students to be sure that they use their own words in their writing. For example, one student researching kangaroos found the following sentence from an Internet source: "Kangaroos can live for months without water." The student, surprised at that fact, started to write it down, but remembering that she needed to use her own words wrote, "Kangaroos can go for a long time without drinking." Kathy's instruction and modeling had an impact.

When the children have finished their reports, they share them by reading them aloud to classmates and taking them home to their parents. Each child has become an "expert" about the topic of the research. (See Figure 27 for a student report on bats of the world.)

As children learn the research techniques using reference tools, they also can learn to use technology to support both their research and their

FIGURE 27

Student Report on Bats of the World

Bats of the World

My favorite animals are bats. Bats are really cool creatures! Here's some cool facts about bats I want to share with you.

Bats look like little furballs with wings. Sometimes they look like birds. Some bats are brown, black, and gray. But no bat looks the same.

Bats live all over the wolrd. But not in really cold or really hot places. Bats live in trees and caves.

Some bats eat blood. Some eat bugs & fish. Did you know this? Some bats even drink necter and pass it like bees!

Their enimies are crocodiles and snakes. They even attack each other sometimes!

Do you know what? Bats are mammals like us! Also bats can't see well. And they hibernate in the winter. Guess what?! Bats have fingers too! The biggest bat is Samoan Flying Fox and the smallest is the Bumble Bee Bat. The Samoan Flying Fox's wingspan is 6½ Feet. Also the vampire bat can help people with heart problems.

Bats are amazing. I'd like to see them in the wild someday.

writing. Children can use computer software programs, such as Kidspiration, to organize their ideas before they start writing. This software program provides templates for various kinds of graphic organizers. Children can move between graphic organizer and text to accomplish their writing. If the class does not have access to Kidspiration, children can use any word-processing software to write their reports. Children also can learn to use presentation software such as PowerPoint to present the information that they have learned through their research.

Renee Miller and Sandy Connor, third-grade teachers in Pennsylvania, have their students do research on the Internet as well as in reference books. When they have completed their research, the children use PowerPoint to present their findings to their classmates and to their parents.

Renee and Sandy find that providing children with appropriate websites is crucial in supporting their students' efforts to find information on the Web. The teachers discuss with students ahead of time the questions that need to be answered and provide them with note-taking sheets for writing down found information. Sandy's students often use print sources for confirming any contradictory information found on websites.

To help the children work with PowerPoint in preparing their presentations, Renee and Sandy provide hard-copy storyboards that are set up in the same format as PowerPoint slides. The children complete the storyboards before they begin working with PowerPoint. This kind of scaffolding prevents the children from being overwhelmed with trying to figure out commands for the program and trying to find accurate information from their notes. Once children have completed their work, they share their presentations with parents, the rest of the class, and the principal.

Written reports also may be done in different formats such as booklets or posters. Renee has her students write reports using a "step book" in which the answers to each of the questions the children have posed and researched are featured in a small booklet. To construct the booklet, three pieces of construction paper are folded at different places so that, when together, each page is slightly different in size and the edges resemble steps. The children then divide their information into logical paragraphs based on the researched questions. Each paragraph is written on a separate page of the booklet and then illustrated. The last page is reserved for information about the author.

Procedural Text

Procedural texts are explanatory in nature and follow a sequence. Examples of procedural text include directions for making something, such as a recipe, or instructions for how to do something, such as playing a game.

As with other types of text, children should have many examples to examine as they work with procedural text. A teacher might use a sample of student work, showing the elements that are usually part of procedure. Bryant and Heard's *Making Shadow Puppets* (2002) provides a good example of procedural text. When children examine this book, they will find that for each chapter, the author lists materials needed, a step-by-step sequence to follow, and diagrams showing what the shadow puppet will look like at each stage.

Another example of procedural text is *How to Make Salsa* (Lucero, 1996), which gives children ideas about how to write recipes. The book lists materials needed and steps to take and includes an informative glossary at the end. Children might want to use the book's format, with its illustrations of ingredients, to write their own recipes. For more advanced readers, *The Sleepover Cookbook* (Warshaw, 2000) provides a different format for recipes but still includes the important ingredients and steps to follow, using photographs rather than illustrations to explain.

After examining several different models, children should be encouraged to identify and list the following characteristics of procedural texts:

Uses directive, imperative language (i.e., do, mix, turn, etc.)

Lists ingredients or implements needed

Offers step-by-step directions

Includes diagrams or pictures of created or end product

Susan Smith (special education teacher) has her students create graphic organizers to indicate the steps for creating something. The students read or listen to text, take notes, and create the graphic organizers prior to making or constructing something. One student who read *Shadow Puppets* (Feely, 1999) created directions on cards before she began making a puppet herself (see Figure 28).

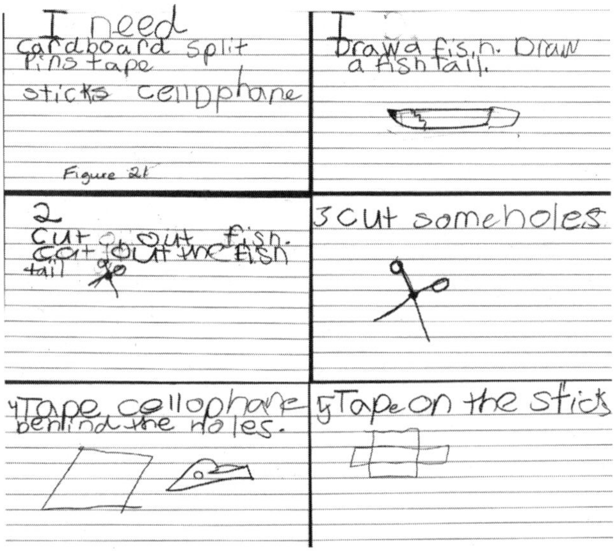

FIGURE 28

Student Procedural Text Using Cards

Kathy Simpson uses a different approach with her second graders. After having identified the components of written instructions, students each choose an activity they feel that they know how to do very well. In a prewriting exercise, they list all the things needed for the described activity, and then they discuss in pairs a good beginning to catch the reader's interest. The students draft their instructions, read them to each other, and then revise and edit them. (See Figure 29 for a student's procedural text about swimming.)

Explanatory Text

Explanatory text is used to explain processes and reasons that things happen. It is often used in describing scientific or social phenomena. It is usually written in sequential order, as is procedural text, but often uses a cause-effect structure (see chapter 5). Explanatory text can be a

FIGURE 29

Student Procedural Text for Swimming

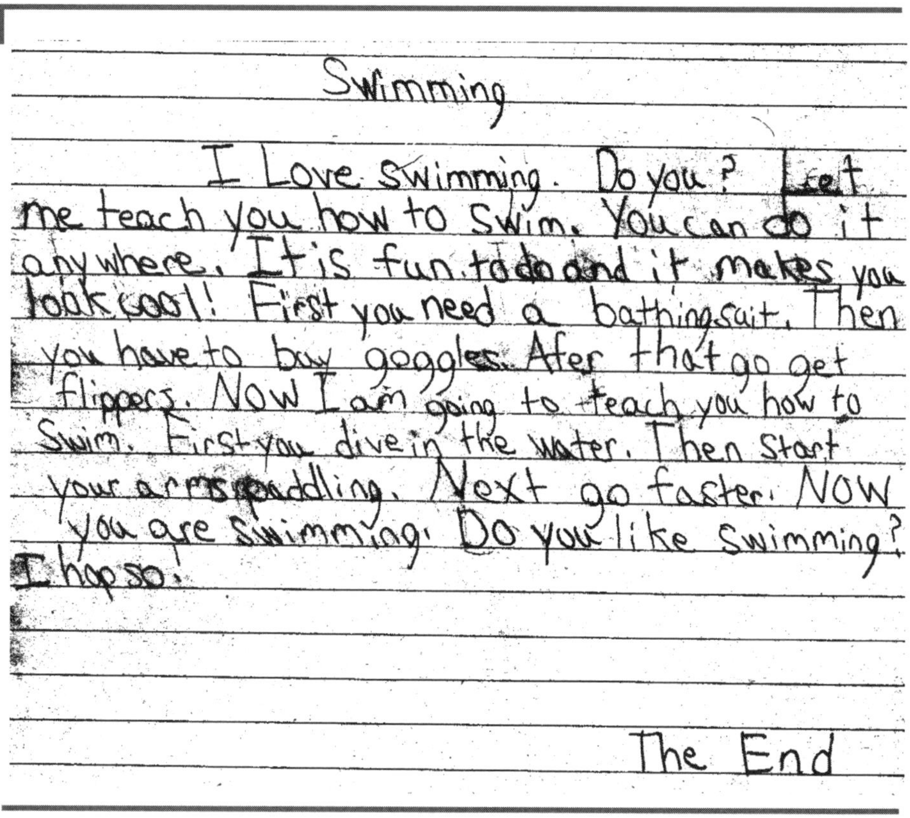

Swimming

I Love swimming. Do you? Let me teach you how to swim. You can do it anywhere. It is fun to do and it makes you look cool! First you need a bathingsuit. Then you have to buy goggles. Afer that go get flippers. Now I am going to teach you how to Swim. First you dive in the water. Then start your arms paddling. Next go faster. NOW you are Swimming. Do you like Swimming? I hop so!

The End

combination of recounts and procedures. For example, after watching caterpillars hatch into butterflies, children might write an explanation of the life cycle of the butterfly. They would be recounting something that happened but also would be putting the steps of the event in sequential order.

Children should examine and discuss a variety of explanatory texts. For example, *From Wax to Crayon* (Nelson, 2003), part of the Start to Finish series, follows the procedure used in making crayons, from melting the wax to sorting the crayons to sending them to the stores. Additional titles in this series explore cotton to T-shirt, kernel to corn, peanut to peanut butter, and tree to paper.

Another example of explanatory text is *What's Happening? A Book of Explanations* (Relf, 2000), which offers multiple explanations complete with drawings. Teachers can use this book as an example of how to include diagrams in explanations; however, children will need guidance with this book because some of the sequences go from right to left instead of the expected left to right.

As children examine explanatory texts, they will learn to identify the following characteristics:

Has a beginning sentence to tell what is being explained

Is written using present tense verbs, indicating the timelessness of the information

Includes the sequence of a process or explanations of characteristics

Offers diagrams or pictures

Has an ending

It is helpful to have children begin writing explanations through shared writing with the teacher about something they have observed. For example, if the class has experimented with things that float or that sink, they could write an explanation about this phenomenon together with the teacher acting as scribe.

To further scaffold their writing, small groups or pairs of children can work to write explanations of things they have observed such as the hatching of chicks or growth of plants. Only after the children have had guided practice with explanatory text should they be expected to write it independently.

Persuasive Text

Persuasive text is written to persuade or convince someone about a particular point of view and usually makes a statement about what the writer wants the reader to believe and then provides reasons or statements that support that view.

According to the 1998 National Assessment of Educational Progress, only 18% of fourth graders were able to score at basic or above levels in writing persuasion (Greenwald, Persky, Campbell, & Mazzeo, 2003). This seems to be the most difficult (or the most neglected) kind of informational writing in K–3 classrooms.

Again, children should examine several examples of persuasive writing before being asked to write in this particular form. Examples can include student writing from previous years or published texts such as *Should We Have Pets? A Persuasive Text* (Lollis, 2003), written by a second-grade class. Children should be able to identify the following characteristics of persuasive text:

Has an opening sentence with an opinion about something

Supports that opinion with reasons

Usually written in present tense (though past tense is not uncommon)

Has an ending sentence restating the opinion

To help children begin writing persuasive texts, Kathy Simpson had her second graders consider an issue for which there were different opinions in the class. She asked the children to think about the four seasons, listing the good things they could think of about each season. After completing the list, each child chose a favorite season and wrote a short, persuasive paragraph using the following format:

I think ______________ is the best season. (The opening sentence giving an opinion)

Write three reasons it is the best season.

So this is why ______________ is the best season.

After children practiced persuasive writing in this structured way, they were better prepared to create their own persuasive pieces. Kathy extended the idea of persuasive writing by having students write letters

FIGURE 30

Example of Student Persuasive Text

Mrs. Simpson I think we should really play Around the wold! We never played it in a long, long, time. Around the world is a good game because it's fun and we lean math. Arond the world is also a good game because we can ether do the clooks or number model. All of us can play, that's another good reason. Am I covincining you? Well that's not even the beginning yet!

Around the world makes math less hard and it's fun too! This will help us with math asinments, triangle facts, and trades first. Their are many jobs that include math for esample, a Sintist he needs to know lots of math! Around the world is a fun math game, now wouden't it be nice to play it?

Serenity

to persuade guests to visit their class. After having successfully persuaded an animal-keeper at the zoo to visit and share his experiences, the children asked Kathy if they could write to other guests persuading them to visit. The persuasive letter became an important part of the classroom culture, which the children also used to try to convince their teacher to use certain classroom activities (see Figure 30).

Writing Frames

A writing frame, which Kathy used for her students' first persuasive writing, is an outline that scaffolds children's attempts to create particular forms of writing. Writing frames provide sentence starters so that children can fill in blanks and have well-developed paragraphs. Children who have difficulty with writing may benefit from the use of writing frames (Wray & Lewis, 1997).

Teachers can develop writing frames for each of the informational text structures (see chapter 5) by using sentence starters and key words. For example, a comparison-contrast frame could start with a sentence: "I read about _____ and ______." The next sentence could tell how the two are alike: "_____ and _____ both _____." Then a sentence (or two) could explain how they are different: "_____ has _____, but _____ has _____." The concluding sentence could be: "_____ and _____ are alike in some ways and different in others." When the children have finished filling out the frame, they have a paragraph written in the comparison-contrast structure. (Figure 31 provides a procedural writing frame.)

When introducing a writing frame, it is important for the teacher to model it with the class as a shared writing. This can be followed by having children complete the frames in pairs. Once children are familiar with the procedure, they can complete the frames independently. As children become used to writing a particular genre, they will no longer need the frames.

FIGURE 31

Procedural Writing Frame

I am going to tell you how to make ____________________.

You need to have ____________________,

____________________,

____________________, and

____________________.

First, you ____________________

____

Then, you ____________________

____

Next, you ____________________

____

Finally, you ____________________

____

Now you have ____________________. Enjoy it!

Poetry as Informational Text

Though most of us do not think of poetry as informational text, children can use poems to write factual information. The poems can be rhyming poems or patterned poems, such as information poems or cinquains. For example, after children have studied a particular topic, they could brainstorm a list of words related to the topic and arrange them in a patterned information poem. For the topic of *fall*, the list of words might include *fall, autumn, falling leaves, cool, raking, school, pumpkins*, or holidays such as *Thanksgiving* or *Halloween*. For an informational poem, children might put one word in the first line, two words in the second line, three words in the third line, and one word in the fourth line:

> Fall
> Halloween, Thanksgiving
> Raking falling leaves
> Autumn

To further enhance young children's creativity and enjoyment, Bromley (2000) suggests making shape books; for example, the above poem could be written on pages in the shape and color of a fall leaf.

Cinquains, with five lines, also could be used to show information about a topic (see Figure 32). Although many teachers use number of

FIGURE 32

Example of Student Cinquain

Shark

Sharp teeth

Swimming in sea

Scaring the scuba divers

Jaws

syllables per line to write cinquains, a simpler version is to use number of words per line. The basic structure is as follows:

> one word (or two syllables) in the first line stating the topic
>
> two words (or four syllables) in the second line describing the topic
>
> three words (or six syllables) in the third line telling an action
>
> four words (or eight syllables) in the fourth line expressing feelings
>
> one word (or two syllables) in the fifth line restating the topic

Poetry, whether rhyming or patterned, provides particularly creative ways of writing information. Poetry may appeal especially to children who enjoy playing with language and to those for whom longer writing assignments are a challenge.

Summary

Reading and writing develop together. As children learn from reading different kinds of informational texts, they also learn to write using the same forms. Children should have opportunities to explore many examples of different forms and to identify their characteristics. Children can learn to write recounts, reports, explanations, procedures, descriptions, and poetry to share information. Writing helps children explore, reorganize, and consolidate their knowledge. In the concluding chapter, we suggest ways to get started with informational text in classrooms.

CHAPTER 8

Putting It All Together

Although primary-grade children traditionally have been exposed to stories almost exclusively, there are compelling reasons to change this situation. First, children's experience cannot be limited to stories if they are to meet current expectations. State and national standards, as well as recommendations of educational organizations, call for young children to handle informational text with facility. Achievement tests for young children include considerable informational text. Further, informational text makes up most of what older children and adults read and write; therefore, it makes sense to give young children the chance to learn about more than stories in school. Second, there are data to support the notion that student achievement will increase with the opportunity to read and receive instruction about informational text. Children whose reading is diverse have higher reading achievement than those who read only stories. Third, informational books and other resources offer great potential for motivating children to read. Indeed, for some children, informational text is the best route for learning to read. Young children typically like informational books and choose to read them as often as stories. And young children have shown that they can handle the demands of informational books. Clearly, children need the opportunity to read and be instructed about both stories and informational text.

Achieving a Balance

To ensure that children experience informational text, we suggest that teachers

- create inviting classroom libraries with lots of informational text, including books, magazines, and Internet resources;

- make informational text an integral part of daily read-alouds;
- teach children comprehension strategies for informational text;
- show children how to find and use information; and
- provide children with experience in informational writing.

These goals will be difficult to accomplish, however, unless children have adequate access to informational text. Because children need to be equally proficient with stories and informational text, we suggest that teachers aim for an equal balance in these materials. Therefore, we recommend that teachers aim for informational texts to be

- 50% of the classroom library,
- 50% of their read-alouds, and
- 50% of their reading instruction.

When aiming for an equal balance, teachers should keep in mind the differences in informational writing. For example, as we discussed in chapter 2, informational books are not all expository. Many informational books for young children are narratives. These narrative-informational books do not afford children the opportunity to read and learn from expository writing. In addition, many informational books for young children are mixed texts that include both narrative and expository writing. With these books, children may attend to the story line while skipping the expository portion. Narrative-informational and mixed texts may also cause children more difficulty in telling fact from fiction than expository books. Because it is important that children experience expository writing—not just story structures—we recommend that teachers limit narrative-informational and mixed texts to no more than one third of their informational book selections. In other words, if half of the material children experience is informational text, then the majority of that should be expository.

Fortunately, there are not only good stories currently available for young children but also many wonderful informational books. Publishers offer an array of beautifully illustrated informational books on wide-ranging topics, and there are many good sources to help locate appropriate books, as we noted in chapter 3. Because so many informational books are available for young children, teachers need not settle for poor examples. Instead, it is important that teachers look for quality books that are written at an appropriate level for the children with whom they will be used. As our guide (see Appendix B, page 129) indicates, informational books should have accurate content, good design, interesting writing, and clear organization.

Getting Started With Informational Text

Read-Alouds

Reading aloud is probably the easiest way to begin using informational books in primary-grade classrooms. Read-alouds enable children to learn the distinctive linguistic features of informational books and to expand their vocabulary and word knowledge. The interaction that occurs during informational book read-alouds promotes meaning seeking and motivates children to read. Further, read-alouds can provide struggling readers with the support they need to read and comprehend a book on their own. Best of all, children enjoy informational book read-alouds.

Read-alouds are perfect vehicles for modeling comprehension strategies that work for informational books, for demonstrating that informational books need not always be read from start to finish, and for showing children how to find information that they want and need. From read-alouds, teachers can move to small-group and whole-class instruction.

As we have noted, we recommend that half of read-alouds be informational text. Teachers can track their read-alouds using a log (see Appendix B, page 131), so that it is easy to see if they are achieving a balance. Children can help teachers record the books and decide which books fall into which category. By doing so, children will increase their understanding of different genres.

Children's Independent Reading

Another easy way to get started with informational books is to encourage students' independent reading. Time to read is important. Teachers should provide time for children to engage in independent reading, and we recommend letting children select what they want to read. However, evidence indicates that when teachers read aloud a book, it increases the likelihood that children will select that book for independent reading. This means that if teachers include informational books in their read-alouds, children will select informational books to read on their own.

Teachers also can influence children's independent reading by having them keep logs of what they read. Even a simple log—with entries for date, title, and author—gives children a concrete record of what they have read. Such a record provides children with tangible evidence of their efforts and helps motivate them to read.

Going beyond a simple log is even more powerful. Dreher (1998/1999) suggests that children keep a log to help them monitor the balance of their reading material. A reading log that calls attention to the genre of books read raises children's awareness of diverse genres and adds to the likelihood that children will seek them out.

There are many possibilities for creating a reading log that highlights different kinds of books. One way is to modify the teacher read-aloud log (see Appendix B, page 131) by giving it a new title, such as "My Reading Record." Children could use it to record the books they read and to check the column for type of book, just as their teachers do for read-alouds.

Another option is to have children record the type of book they read with a color code (see Appendix C, page 136). Teachers and students can devise their own color system. For example, one third-grade class used the following system:

Color	Type of Reading
Blue	Fiction
Red	Biography
Orange	How to do it
Green	Social studies
Purple	Science
Black	Poetry
Brown	Other

Children in that class helped put color-coded stickers on the books in their classroom library to make the various types easy to find. Other teachers and students may wish to choose simpler color codes, perhaps using only the categories of fiction, narrative-informational, expository, and mixed text.

Moving Forward With Informational Text

Once teachers are at ease with informational text in read-alouds and independent reading, they can extend their efforts. As we have noted, it is important to include informational text in reading instruction and to include reading instruction in content areas. Young children also need opportunities to read and learn from informational text in magazines and newspapers, to search for information not only in books but also on the Internet, and to engage in informational writing about what they have learned.

As teachers infuse their instruction with informational text, it is important that they keep certain points in mind.

First, stories are important too. We do not suggest eliminating them, only that informational text be given equal attention.

Second, the recommendations we have made in this book should not simply be added on to what is already going in school. Instead, practices will need to be adjusted rather than expanded. For instance, teachers can replace some of the stories used in reading instruction with informational text. Reading instruction can occur in content areas—not just during reading. Similarly, some story writing can be replaced with informational writing.

Third, informational text should be used in meaningful contexts. We do not recommend isolated exercises in finding information or practicing comprehension strategies. Strategies for informational text should be taught in real reading situations. The focus should be on the meaningful task at hand, not on using strategies for their own sake. When modeling, guided practice, and gradual transfer of responsibility occur in real reading situations, children are much more likely to learn what is being taught and to develop the flexibility that will let them apply what they have learned in other contexts.

Finally, all children benefit from the opportunity to experience informational text along with stories. The examples in this book come from children and teachers in schools across the full range of achievement levels, including schools in high-poverty areas as well as those in more fortunate areas. Whether they are struggling readers and writers, or average and advanced readers and writers, children respond well and learn much from literacy experiences that include informational text.

Informational books and other informational text offer rich opportunities to primary-grade children and their teachers. We have presented many possibilities. Creative primary-grade teachers will come up with many more.

APPENDIX

Resources for Teachers

Children's Magazines and Newspapers Featuring Informational Text

Appleseeds
Cobblestone Publishing
A Division of Carus Publishing Company
30 Grove Street, Ste. C
Peterborough, NH 03458, USA
Tel. 800-821-0115
www.cobblestonepub.com

Aimed at children ages 8 and up. Each issue focuses on a social studies theme.

ASK
Cobblestone Publishing
A Division of Carus Publishing Company
30 Grove Street, Ste. C
Peterborough, NH 03458, USA
Tel. 800-821-0115
www.cobblestonepub.com

Aimed at children ages 6 to 9. ASK stands for Arts and Sciences for Kids. Each issue focuses on a theme.

chickaDEE and OWL
25 Boxwood Lane
Buffalo, NY 14227-2707, USA
Tel. 800-551-6957
www.owlkids.com
In Canada:
OWL
PO Box 726
Markham Station, Markham
ON Canada L3P 7V9

chickaDEE is for children ages 6 to 9. Includes hands-on science activities. OWL is for children ages 9 to 13. Features amazing facts and the science behind how things work.

Click
A Division of Carus Publishing Company
Cricket Magazine Group
PO Box 9306
LaSalle, IL 61301, USA
Tel. 800-821-0115
www.cricketmag.com

For children ages 3 to 7. Features science and exploration.

Kids Discover
149 Fifth Avenue
New York, NY 10010, USA
Tel. 212-677-4457
www.kidsdiscover.com

Aimed at ages 6 and up. Features history, nature, science, and geography. Each issue focuses on one topic.

National Geographic for Kids
PO Box 63002
Tampa, FL 33663-3002, USA
Tel. 800-647-5463
www.nationalgeographic.com/education

Aimed at children in grades 3–6. Formerly titled *World*. Features articles and photos on geography, science, nature, and social studies.

Ranger Rick
National Wildlife Federation
PO Box 2038
Harlan, IA 51593, USA
Tel. 800-611-1599
www.nwf.org/kids

For children ages 7 to 12. Focuses on nature, with animal photos, information, and stories.

Scholastic News
Scholastic Magazines
PO Box 3710
Jefferson City, MO 65102, USA
Tel. 800-724-6527
http://teacher.scholastic.com/products/classmags/index.htm

Available in separate editions for grades 1, 2, and 3. Features news and current events.

Sports Illustrated for Kids
PO Box 60001
Tampa, FL 33660, USA
Tel. 800-462-1661
www.sikids.com

For children ages 8 to 15. Features sports news and articles and related photos. Most appropriate for the oldest primary-grade children.

TIME for Kids
PO Box 60001
Tampa, FL 33600, USA
Tel. 800-777-8600
www.timeforkids.com

Available in separate editions for each grade level: *Big Picture* is for grades K–1 and *News Scoop* is for grades 2–3. Features world and national news, sports, entertainment, and current events, and games.

Weekly Reader
200 Stamford Place
PO Box 120023
Stamford, CT 06912-0023, USA
Tel. 800-446-3355
www.weeklyreader.com

Available in separate editions for grades pre–K, K, 1, 2, and 3. Features world and national news and current events.

YES Mag: Canada's Science Magazine for Kids
3968 Long Gun Place
Victoria, BC
Canada V8N 3A9
www.yesmag.bc.ca

For children ages 8 to14. Features general science, technology, engineering, and mathematics, including "do-at-home" projects.

Your Big Backyard
National Wildlife Federation
PO Box 2038
Harlan, IA 51593, USA
Tel. 800-611-1599
www.nwf.org/kids

For children ages 3 to 7. Focuses on nature with animal photos, information, and stories.

Zoobooks
Wildlife Education Ltd.
12233 Thatcher Court
Poway, CA 92064, USA
Tel. 800-992-5034
www.zoobooks.com

For children ages 4 to 11. Contains facts and photos about specific animals and animal groups.

Websites for Lists of Informational Books

Organization	List	Characteristics	Website
International Reading Association	Children's Choices Teachers' Choices	Includes informational books and story books	www.reading.org
Children's Book Council	Children's Choices Outstanding Science Trade Books for Children Notable Children's Trade Books in the Field of Social Studies Caldecott Medal Books Newbery Medal Books Robert F. Sibert Information Book Award	General source for many different book lists	www.cbcbooks.org
National Council of Teachers of English	Orbis Pictus Award for Outstanding Nonfiction for Children	Given yearly to outstanding informational book; honor books also listed with annotations	www.ncte.org
National Science Teachers Association	Outstanding Science Trade Books for Children	Provides annotations and suggested grade levels	www.nsta.org

(continued)

Websites for Lists of Informational Books *(continued)*

Organization	List	Characteristics	Website
National Council for the Social Studies	Notable Children's Trade Books in the Field of Social Studies	Provides annotations and suggested grade levels; divided into social studies themes	www.socialstudies.org
The Association for Library Services to Children	Robert F. Sibert Information Book Award Caldecott Medal Books Newbery Medal Books	Award-winning books	www.ala.org
Northeastern University	Appraisal: Science Books for Young People	Quarterly online publication with reviews by librarians and scientists	www.appraisal.neu.edu
Heinemann	Search It! Science	Book reviews by educators	www.Searchit.heinemann.com
University of Maryland, Baltimore County	The Elementary Science Integration Projects	Science lesson plans and suggested books for K–8	www.umbc.edu/esip

Strategy Instruction Plan

I. Introduce the text to engage students' curiosity and probe for prior knowledge
   a. by pictures
   b. by anecdote
   c. by questions (such as Did you know that...?)

II. Introduce strategy
   a. explain what it is
   b. explain how to do it
   c. explain when it is useful

III. Provide modeling of the strategy
   a. use first part of text
   b. explain what you are doing as you use the strategy

IV. Provide guided practice
   a. use next section of text
   b. encourage children to join you using the strategy
   c. provide feedback
   d. don't expect all children to pick up the strategy at the same time
   e. realize that as the children are focusing on using the strategy, their comprehension may initially suffer

V. Provide scaffolded independent practice
   a. use a different text
   b. encourage children to use the strategy in small groups or pairs
   c. provide feedback

VI. Provide independent practice
   a. encourage children to use the strategy as they read different texts
   b. discuss whether strategy would be effective for different materials
   c. continue talking about the strategy throughout the year

VII. Always keep strategy instruction in purposeful, authentic reading activities

Common Informational Text Structures

Text Structure	Definition	Signal Words
cause–effect	describes causes of certain events	because, cause, if, so, as a result of, since, in order to
comparison–contrast	tells how two or more things are alike or different	different from, like, compared to, similar to, alike, same as, on the other hand
sequence	explains something in time order	first, next, then, finally, last, all number words
description	gives characteristics	color, size, etc.
problem–solution	presents a problem and suggests a solution	problem, because, cause, solution, so, so that, in order to, since
question–answer	presents a question and gives answers	who, what, why, when, where, how
generalization–example	gives a general statement and provides examples	for example

Types and Characteristics of Informational Writing

Recount	Report	Procedure	Explanation	Persuasion
Past tense	Written using present-tense verbs indicating the timelessness of the information	Imperative (understood to be directly addressing "you") Example: [You] mix two cups of flour.	Written using present-tense verbs indicating the timelessness of the information but can also have past tense	Written using present-tense verbs indicating the timelessness of the information but can also have past tense
Based on personal experience	Based on research and experience	Based on research or experience	Based on research or experience	Based on research, experience, and personal opinion
Beginning sentence to tell what it is about and to interest reader	Beginning sentence to tell what the report is about and to interest reader	Beginning sentence to tell what the procedure is	Beginning sentence to tell what the explanation is about	Beginning sentence that presents what the writer wants the reader to believe
Written in the order the experience happened	Organized according to topic Has factual information Often has pictures or diagrams for illustration	States materials needed Written in a step-by-step order Often has pictures or diagrams	Written in a step-by-step order Often has pictures or diagrams	Organized by arguments
Closing sentence	Closing sentence summarizing the report	Closing sentence describing the outcome	Closing sentence indicating the end of the process explained	Closing sentence stating what the writer wants the reader to believe

APPENDIX

B

Forms for Teachers

Checklist for a Well-Designed K–3 Classroom Library

Characteristic	Yes	Making Progress	No
Range of informational text, with lots of expository text			
Range of fiction			
50/50 balance of informational text/fiction			
Variety of reading levels			
At least 8 books per child			
New books added regularly			
Multiple copies of some titles			
Face out presentation of many books			
Simple method for checking materials in and out			
Quiet and well-lit			
Seating and/or carpeting			
Partitioned on at least 2 sides			
Books organized in some method			
Flannel board /props/writing materials			
Large enough for at least 5 children at a time			
Assortment of magazines			
Books on tape/computer with headsets			
Internet access			

Adapted from Fractor et al. (1993) and Morrow (1991), as well as our own suggestions.

Guide for Choosing Informational Books

Name of Book ____________________ Type of Book ____________________

Characteristic	Notes	Possible Instruction
Content Accuracy		
Author's and illustrator's qualifications • Experts in field • "Insiders" (if multicultural book) • Award-winning		
References used • Consultants who are experts • Print sources		
Information current • Copyright date recent (if important) • Information up to date		
Distinguishes between fact and theory • Clear what is believed and what is known		
Text and illustrations clear		
Stereotypes not used in text or illustration		
Design		
Illustrations appropriate for content		
Illustrations well placed on the page		
Clear about where to begin reading		
Illustrations labeled and explained		
Captions clear and informative		
Relative sizes indicated • Enlargements noted		

(continued)

Guide for Choosing Informational Books *(continued)*

Name of Book ____________________ Type of Book ____________________

Characteristic	Notes	Possible Instruction
Style		
Lively, engaging language		
Accurate terminology used		
Appropriate for children's level		
Generalizations and concepts given (not just a collection of facts)		
Enthusiasm for topic evident		
Organization		
Informational book characteristics • Pagination, table of contents, index, glossary, additional reading list		
Headings and subheadings		
Clear pattern of organization		

Read-Aloud Log

		Type of Book			
			Informational Books		
Date	**Author/Title**	**Fiction**	**Expository-Informational**	**Mixed**	**Narrative-Informational**

Adapted from Dreher & Baker (2003).

APPENDIX

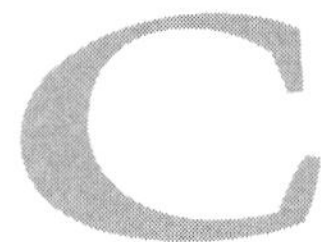

Forms for Students

Questions to Monitor Information Searches

Question	Yes	No
What information do I need?		
Does this book (or website or magazine) have search features that would help me find what I want to know?		
Is the information that I need located here?		
Does the information I have located make sense?		
Is there anything in this book (or website or magazine) to help me decide if the information is correct?		
Does this information relate to things I already know?		
Do I have all the information that I need to answer my question? If not, I should continue searching.		

Adapted from Dreher (1992).

Report Note-Taking Sheet

What I want to learn:

What I already know:

What I learned:

Report Checklist

1. My title tells what the report is about.
2. My first sentence tells what the report is about and has something interesting to make someone want to read it.
3. My facts are written in sentences and are in my own words.
4. I have enough facts in my report to make it interesting for someone else to read.
5. I have grouped my sentences into paragraphs that make sense.
6. I have a good ending that wraps up my report.
7. I have a picture, diagram, or chart to help make my report clear.
8. I have checked my spelling and punctuation.
9. The part I like best is ________________________________.

Based on ideas from Kathy Simpson.

My Reading Log

Name ______________________________

Date	Title	Author	Type (Color Code*)

**Teachers and students can create and post a color key for type of book.*

Alexander, P.A. (1997). Knowledge-seeking and self-schema: A case for the motivational dimensions of exposition. *Educational Psychologist, 32*, 83–94.

American Association of School Librarians. (1998). *Information power: Building partnerships for learning*. Chicago: American Library Association.

Anderson, R.C., Wilson, P.T., & Fielding, L.G. (1988). Growth in reading and how children spend their time outside of school. *Reading Research Quarterly, 23*, 285–303.

Baker, L., & Wigfield, A. (1999). Dimensions of children's motivation for reading and their relations to reading activity and reading achievement. *Reading Research Quarterly, 34*, 452–477.

Beck, I.L., McKeown, M.G., Sandora, D., & Worthy, J. (1996). Questioning the author: A yearlong classroom implementation to engage students with text. *The Elementary School Journal, 96*, 385–414.

Bednar, M.R., & Kletzien, S.B. (1993). Beyond the techniques: Strategic content readers. *The Reading Instruction Journal, 36*, 4–11.

Brabham, E., Boyd, P., & Edgington, W.D. (2000). Sorting it out: Students' responses to fact and fiction in informational storybooks as read-alouds for science and social studies. *Reading Research and Instruction, 39*, 265–290.

British Columbia Department of Education. (2002). British Columbia performance standards. Retrieved April 22, 2003, from http://www.bced.gov.bc.ca/perf_stands/reading.htm

Britt, G., & Baker, L. (1997). *Engaging parents and kindergartners in reading through class lending library* (Instructional Resource No. 41). University of Georgia, Athens, and University of Maryland, College Park: National Reading Research Center. (ERIC Document Reproduction Service No. ED405553)

Bromley, K. (2000). Teaching young children to be writers. In D.S. Strickland & L.M. Morrow (Eds.), *Beginning reading and writing* (pp. 111–120). New York: Teachers College Press; Newark, DE: International Reading Association.

Brown, A.L., Campione, J.C., & Day, J. D. (1981). Learning to learn: On training students to learn from texts. *Educational Researcher, 10*, 14–21.

Brown, A.L., & Palincsar, A.S. (1985). *Reciprocal teaching of comprehension strategies: A natural history of one program for enhancing learning* (Technical Report No. 334). Urbana, IL: University of Illinois, Center for the Study of Reading.

Brown, R., Pressley, M., Van Meter, P., & Schuder, T. (1996). A quasi-experimental validation of transactional strategies instruction with low-achieving second grade readers. *Journal of Educational Psychology, 88*, 18–37.

Buss, K., & Karnowski, L. (2000). *Reading and writing literary genres*. Newark, DE: International Reading Association.

Calkins, L.M., Montgomery, K., Santman, D., & Falk, B. (1998). *A teacher's guide to standardized reading tests*. Portsmouth, NH: Heinemann.

Camp, D. (2000). It takes two: Teaching with twin texts of fact and fiction. *The Reading Teacher*, *53*, 400–408.

Campbell, J.R., Kapinus, B.A., & Beatty, A.S. (1995). *Interviewing children about their literacy experiences: Data from NAEP's Integrated Reading Performance Record (IRPR) at Grade 4*. Washington, DC: National Center for Educational Statistics.

Caswell, L.J., & Duke, N.K. (1998). Non-narrative as a catalyst for literacy development. *Language Arts*, *75*, 108–117.

Chambliss, M.J., & McKillop, A.M. (2000). Creating a print- and technology-rich classroom library to entice children to read. In L. Baker, M.J. Dreher, & J.T. Guthrie (Eds.), *Engaging young readers: Promoting achievement and motivation* (pp. 94–118). New York: Guilford.

Coles, M., & Hall, C. (2002). Gendered readings: Learning from children's reading choices. *Journal of Research in Reading*, *25*, 96–108.

Copenhaver, J.F. (2001). Running out of time: Rushed read-alouds in a primary classroom. *Language Arts*, *79*, 148–158.

Donovan, C.A., Smolkin, L.B., & Lomax, R.G. (2000). Beyond the independent-level text: Considering the reader-text match in first graders' self-selections during recreational reading. *Reading Psychology*, *21*, 309–333.

Dreher, M.J. (1992). Locating information in textbooks. *Journal of Reading*, *35*, 364–371.

Dreher, M.J. (1998/1999). Motivating children to read more nonfiction. *The Reading Teacher*, *52*, 414–417.

Dreher, M.J. (2000). Fostering reading for learning. In L. Baker, M.J. Dreher, & J.T. Guthrie (Eds.), *Engaging young readers: Promoting achievement and motivation* (pp. 68–93). New York: Guilford.

Dreher, M.J. (2002). Children searching and using information text: A critical part of comprehension. In C.C. Block & M. Pressley (Eds.), *Comprehension instruction: Research-based best practices* (pp. 289–304). New York: Guilford.

Dreher, M.J. (2003). Motivating struggling readers by tapping the potential of information books. *Reading & Writing Quarterly*, *19*, 25–38.

Dreher, M.J., & Baker, L. (2003). *Balancing learning to read and reading for learning: Achievement and engagement in young children's reading instruction*. Unpublished manuscript.

Dreher, M.J., & Dromsky, A. (2000, December). *Increasing the diversity of young children's independent reading*. Paper presented at the National Reading Conference, Scottsdale, AZ.

Dreher, M.J., & Sammons, R.B. (1994). Fifth-graders' search for information in a textbook. *Journal of Reading Behavior*, *26*, 301–314.

Dreher, M.J., & Voelker, A. (in press). Science books for primary-grade classrooms: The importance of balance and quality. In W. Saul (Ed.), *Crossing borders in literacy and science instruction: Perspectives on theory and practice*. Newark, DE: International Reading Association.

Duffy, G.G. (2002). The case for direct explanation of strategies. In C.C. Block & M. Pressley (Eds.), *Comprehension instruction: Research-based best practices* (pp. 28–41). New York: Guilford.

Duke, N.K. (2000). 3.6 minutes per day: The scarcity of informational texts in first grade. *Reading Research Quarterly*, *35*, 202–224.

Duke, N.K., & Kays, J. (1998). "Can I say 'Once upon a time'?": Kindergarten children developing knowledge of information book language. *Early Childhood Research Quarterly*, *13*, 295–318.

Duke, N.K., & Pearson, P.D. (2002). Effective practices for developing reading comprehension. In A.E. Farstrup & S.J. Samuels (Eds.), *What research has to say about reading instruction* (3rd ed., pp. 205–242). Newark: DE: International Reading Association.

El-Dinary, P.B. (2002). Challenges of implementing transactional strategies instruction for reading comprehension. In C.C. Block & M. Pressley (Eds.), *Comprehension instruction: Research-based best practices* (pp. 201–215). New York: Guilford.

Elley, W.B. (1992). *How in the world do students read?* Hamburg, Germany: International Association for the Evaluation of Educational Achievement.

Feitelson, P., Kita, D., & Goldstein, Z. (1986). Effects of listening to series stories on first graders' comprehension and use of language. *Research in Teaching of English*, *20*, 339–356.

Feldt, R.C., Feldt, R.A., & Kilburg, K. (2002). Acquisition, maintenance, and transfer of a questioning strategy in second- and third-grade students to learn from science textbooks. *Reading Psychology*, *23*, 181–198.

Fielding, L., & Roller, C. (1992). Making difficult books accessible and easy books acceptable. *The Reading Teacher*, *45*, 678–685.

Fractor, J.S., Woodruff, M.C., Martinez, M.G., & Teale, W.H. (1993). Let's not miss opportunities to promote voluntary reading: Classroom libraries in the elementary school. *The Reading Teacher*, *46*, 476–484.

Fredericks, A.D. (1986). Mental imagery activities to improve comprehension. *The Reading Teacher*, *40*, 78–81.

Freedman, R. (1992). Fact or fiction? In E.B. Freeman & D.G. Person (Eds.), *Using nonfiction trade books in the elementary classroom* (pp. 2–10). Urbana, IL: National Council of Teachers of English.

Greenwald, E.A., Persky, H.R., Campbell, J.R., & Mazzeo, J. (2002). *The nation's report card, NAEP 1998 writing report card for the nation and the states*. Retrieved May 14, 2003, from http://nces.ed.gov/nationsreportcard

Hiebert, E.H., & Fisher, C.W. (1990). Whole language: Three themes for the future. *Educational Leadership*, *47*, 62–64.

Hiebert, E.H., & Raphael, T.E. (1998). *Early literacy instruction*. New York: Harcourt Brace.

Hoffman, J.V. (1992). Critical reading/thinking across the curriculum: Using I-charts to support learning. *Language Arts*, *69*, 121–127.

Hoffman, J.V., Roser, N.L., & Battle, J. (1993). Reading aloud in classrooms: From modal to a "model." *The Reading Teacher*, *46*, 496–505.

Horowitz, R., & Freeman, S.H. (1995). Robots versus spaceships: The role of discussion in kindergartners' and second graders' preferences for science texts. *The Reading Teacher*, *49*, 30–40.

Hynes, M. (2000). "I read for facts": Reading nonfiction in a fictional world. *Language Arts*, *77*, 485–495.

International Reading Association. (1999). *Providing books and other print materials for classroom and school libraries* (A position statement of the International Reading Association). Newark, DE: Author.

International Reading Association (IRA), & National Association for the Education of Young Children (NAEYC). (1998). *Learning to read and write: Developmentally appropriate practices for young children* (A position statement of IRA & NAEYC). Newark, DE: Authors.

Jacobs, J.S., Morrison, T.G., & Swinyard, W.R. (2000). Reading aloud to students: A national probability study of classroom reading practices of elementary school teachers. *Reading Psychology*, *21*, 171–193.

Jetton, T. (1994). Information-driven versus story-driven: What children remember when they are read informational stories. *Reading Psychology*, *15*, 109–130.

Kamil, M.L., & Lane, D. (1997, December). *Using information text for first-grade reading instruction*. Paper presented at the annual meeting of National Reading Conference, Scottsdale, AZ.

Kamil, M.L., & Lane, D. (1998, December). *Informational text, reading instruction and demands of technology in elementary school*. Paper presented at the annual meeting of the National Reading Conference, Austin, TX.

Kane, S. (1998). The view from the discourse level: Teaching relationships and text structure. *The Reading Teacher*, *52*, 182–184.

Kintsch, W., & Van Dijk, T.A. (1978). Toward a model of text comprehension and production. *Psychological Review*, *85*, 363–394.

Kletzien, S.B. (1991). Strategy use by good and poor comprehenders reading expository text of differing levels. *Reading Research Quarterly*, *26*, 67–86.

Kletzien, S.B. (1992). Proficient and less proficient comprehenders' strategy use for different top-level structures. *Journal of Reading Behavior, 24,* 191–215.

Kletzien, S.B., & DeRenzi, A. (2001, December). "I like real books": Children's genre preferences. Paper presented at the annual meeting of the National Reading Conference, San Antonio, TX.

Kletzien, S.B., & Szabo, R. (1998, December). *Information text or narrative text? Children's preferences revisited.* Paper presented at the annual meeting of the National Reading Conference, Austin, TX.

Korkeamäki, R., Tiainen, O., & Dreher, M.J. (1998). Helping Finnish second-graders make sense of their reading and writing in science projects. In T. Shanahan & F.V. Rodriguez-Brown (Eds.), *47th yearbook of the National Reading Conference* (pp. 334–344). Chicago: National Reading Conference.

Krashen, S. (1995). School libraries, public libraries, and the NAEP reading scores. *School Library Media Quarterly, 23,* 235–238.

Leu, D.J., Jr. (2000). Literacy and technology: Deictic consequences for literacy education in an Information Age. In M.L. Kamil, P.B. Mosenthal, P.D. Pearson, & R. Barr (Eds.), *Handbook of reading research* (Vol. 3, pp. 743–770). Mahwah, NJ: Erlbaum.

Leu, D.J., Jr. (2002). The new literacies: Research on reading instruction with the Internet and other digital technologies. In A.E. Farstrup & S.J. Samuels (Eds.), *What research has to say about reading instruction* (3rd ed., pp. 310–336). Newark, DE: International Reading Association.

Littlefair, A. (1991). *Reading all types of writing.* Buckingham, UK: Open University Press.

Mallett, M. (1999). *Young researchers: Informational reading and writing in the early and primary years.* London: Routledge.

Martinez, M.G., Roser, N.L., Worthy, J., Strecker, S., & Gough, P. (1997). Classroom libraries and children's book selections: Redefining "access" in self-selected reading. In C.K. Kinzer, K.A. Hinchman, & D.J. Leu (Eds.), *Inquiries in literacy theory and practice* (46th yearbook of the National Reading Conference, pp. 265–272). Chicago: National Reading Conference.

Mayer, D.A. (1995). How can we best use children's literature in teaching science concepts? *Science and Children, 32,* 16–19, 43.

McGill-Franzen, A., Allington, R.L., Yokoi, L., & Brooks, G. (1999). Putting books in the classroom seems necessary but not sufficient. *Journal of Educational Research, 93,* 67–74.

Meyer, B.J.F., Brandt, D.M., & Bluth, G.J. (1980). Use of top-level structure in text: Key for reading comprehension of ninth-grade students. *Reading Research Quarterly, 16,* 72–103.

Morrow, L.M. (1991). Promoting voluntary reading. In J. Flood, J.M. Jensen, D. Lapp, & J.R. Squire (Eds.), *Handbook of research on teaching the English language arts* (pp. 681–690). New York: Macmillan.

Moss, B., & Newton, E. (1998, December). *An examination of the informational text genre in recent basal readers*. Paper presented at the annual meeting of the National Reading Conference, Austin, TX.

Moss, G. (2001). To work or play? Junior age non-fiction as objects of design. *Reading, 35*, 106–110.

National Commission on Writing in America's Schools and Colleges. (2003). *The neglected "R": The need for a writing revolution*. New York: College Entrance Examination Board. Retrieved May 14, 2003, from http://www.writingcommission.org

National Institute of Child Health and Human Development (NICHD). (2000). *Report of the National Reading Panel. Teaching children to read: An evidence-based assessment of the scientific research literature on reading and its implications for reading instruction* (NIH Publication No. 00-4769). Washington, DC: U.S. Government Printing Office.

Neuman, S.B. (1999). Books make a difference: A study of access to literacy. *Reading Research Quarterly, 34*, 286–311.

Neuman, S.B., & Celano, D. (2001). Access to print in low-income and middle-income communities. *Reading Research Quarterly, 36*, 8–26.

Ogle, D. (1986). K-W-L: A teaching model that develops active reading of expository text. *The Reading Teacher, 40*, 564–570.

Oyler, C. (1996). Sharing authority: Student initiations during teacher-led read-alouds of information books. *Teaching & Teacher Education, 12*, 149–160.

Oyler, C., & Barry, A. (1996). Intertextual connections in read-alouds of information books. *Language Arts, 73*, 324–329.

Palincsar, A.S., & Brown, A.L. (1989). Instruction for self-regulated reading. In L.B. Resnick & L.E. Klopfer (Eds.), *Toward the thinking curriculum: Current cognitive research* (pp. 19–39). Alexandria, VA: Association for Supervision and Curriculum Development.

Pappas, C.C. (1991). Young children's strategies in learning the "book language" of information books. *Discourse Processes, 14*, 208–225.

Pappas, C.C. (1993). Is narrative "primary"? Some insights from kindergartners' pretend readings of stories and information books. *Journal of Reading Behavior, 25*, 97–129.

Pappas, C.C., & Barry, A. (1997). Scaffolding urban students' initiations: Transactions in reading information books in the read-aloud curriculum genre. In N.J. Karolides (Ed.), *Reader response in elementary classrooms: Quest and discovery* (pp. 215–236). Mahwah, NJ: Erlbaum.

Pappas, C.C., Varelas, M., Barry, A., & O'Neill, A. (2000, December). *The development of science discourse genres in a primary-grade integrated science-literacy unit on states of matter: Analysis of intertextuality*. Paper presented at the annual meeting of the National Reading Conference, Scottsdale, AZ.

Pearson, P.D., & Duke, N.K. (2002). Comprehension instruction in the primary grades. In C.C. Block & M. Pressley (Eds.), *Comprehension instruction: Research-based best practices* (pp. 247–258). New York: Guilford.

Pennsylvania Department of Education. (2003). *Academic standards for reading, writing, speaking and listening*. Retrieved April 23, 2003, from http://www.pde.state.pa.us/k12

Pressley, M., Dolezal, S.E., Raphael, L.M., Mohan, L., Roehrig, A.D., & Bogner, K. (2003). *Motivating primary-grade students*. New York: Guilford.

Pressley, M., Rankin, J., & Yokoi, L. (1996). A survey of instructional practices of primary teachers nominated as effective in promoting literacy. *The Elementary School Journal*, *96*, 363–384.

Rice, D.C. (2002). Using trade books in teaching elementary science: Facts and fallacies. *The Reading Teacher*, *55*, 552–565.

Richgels, D.J., McGee, L.M., Lomax, R.G., & Sheard, C. (1987). Awareness of four text structures: Effects on recall of expository text. *Reading Research Quarterly*, *25*, 80–89.

Roller, C.M. (1990). The interaction between knowledge and structure variables in the processing of expository prose. *Reading Research Quarterly*, *25*, 80–89.

Rosenhouse, J., Feitelson, D., Kita, B., & Goldstein, Z. (1997). Interactive reading aloud to Israeli first graders: Its contribution to literacy development. *Reading Research Quarterly*, *32*, 168–183.

Sanacore, J. (1991). Expository and narrative text: Balancing young children's reading experiences. *Childhood Education*, *67*, 211–214.

Shiel, G. (2001/2002). Reforming reading instruction in Ireland and England. *The Reading Teacher*, *55*, 372–374.

Smith, C., Constantino, R., & Krashen, S. (1997, March/April). Differences in print environment for children in Beverly Hills, Compton and Watts. *Emergency Librarian*, *24*, 8–9.

Smolkin, L., & Donovan, C. (2001). The contexts of comprehension: The information book read aloud, comprehension acquisition, and comprehension instruction in a first-grade classroom. *The Elementary School Journal*, *102*, 97–122.

Snow, C.E., Burns, M.S., & Griffin, P. (Eds.). (1998). *Preventing reading difficulties in young children*. Washington, DC: National Academy Press.

Stauffer, R.G. (1975). *Directing the reading-thinking process*. New York: Harper & Row.

Stead, T. (2002). *Is that a fact? Teaching nonfiction writing K–3*. Portland, ME: Stenhouse.

Sticht, T.G., & James, J.H. (1984). Listening and reading. In P.D. Pearson, R. Barr, M.L. Kamil, & P.B. Mosenthal (Eds.), *Handbook of reading research* (pp. 293–318). New York: Longman.

Sutherland, Z., Monson, D.L., & Arbuthnot, M.H. (1981). *Children and books* (6th ed.). Glenview, IL: Scott, Foresman.

Taylor, B.M., Frye, B.J., & Maruyama, G.M. (1990). Time spent reading and reading growth. *American Educational Research Journal*, *27*, 351–362.

Van den Broek, P., & Kremer, K.E. (2000). The mind in action: What it means to comprehend. In B.M. Taylor, M.F. Graves, & P. Van den Broek (Eds.), *Reading for meaning: Fostering comprehension in the middle grades* (pp. 1–31). New York: Teachers College Press; Newark, DE: International Reading Association.

Venezky, R.L. (2000). The origins of the present-day chasm between adult literacy needs and school literacy instruction. *Scientific Studies of Reading*, *4*, 19–39.

Virginia Department of Education. (2003). Revised English Standards of learning curriculum framework K–grade 5 (Adopted February 26, 2003). Retrieved April 23, 2003, from http://www.pen.k12.va.us/vDOE/Instruction/English/ElemEnglishCF

Walpole, S. (1998/1999). Changing texts, changing thinking: Comprehension demands of new science textbooks. *The Reading Teacher*, *52*, 358–369.

Warren, L., & Fitzgerald, J. (1997). Helping parents to read expository literature to their children: Promoting main idea and detail understanding. *Reading Research and Instruction*, *36*, 342–350.

Wisconsin Department of Public Instruction. (2003). *Wisconsin reading comprehension test*. Retrieved April 23, 2003, from http://www.dpi.state.wi.us/oea/wrctinfo.html#contwrct

Worthy, J., Moorman, M., & Turner, M. (1999). What Johnny likes to read is hard to find in school. *Reading Research Quarterly*, *34*, 12–27.

Wray, D., & Lewis, M. (1997). *Extending literacy: Children reading and writing non-fiction*. New York: Routledge.

Wray, D., & Lewis, M. (1998). An approach to factual writing. *Reading Online*. Retrieved April 23, 2003, from http://www.readingonline.org

Aliki. (1974). *Milk: From cow to carton*. New York: HarperCollins.

Balance, A. (2000). *Deserts*. Carlsbad, CA: Dominie Press.

Balance, A. (2002). *Thieves & rascals*. Carlsbad, CA: Dominie Press.

Balestrino, P. (1989). *The skeleton inside you* (Rev. ed.). Ill. T. Kelley. New York: HarperCollins.

Barrett, J. (1978). *Cloudy with a chance of meatballs*. Ill. R. Barrett. New York: Atheneum.

Brenner, B. (1997). *Thinking about ants*. Ill. C. Schwartz. Greenvale, NY: Mondo.

Brown, D. (1993). *Ruth Law thrills a nation*. Boston: Houghton Mifflin.

Bryant, J., & Heard, C. (2002). *Making shadow puppets*. Tonawanda, NY: Kids Can Press.

Calmenson, S. (2001). *Rosie: A visiting dog's story*. Boston: Houghton Mifflin.

Carle, E. (1975). *The mixed-up chameleon*. New York: Scholastic.

Clarke, B. (1990). *Amazing Frogs & Toads*. Photo. J. Young. New York: Knopf.

Cohn, A.L., & Schmidt, S. (2002). *Abraham Lincoln*. Ill. D.A. Johnson. New York: Scholastic.

Cole, J. (1986). *Hungry, hungry sharks*. Ill. P. Wynne. New York: Random House.

Cole, J. (1990). *The Magic School Bus: Inside the human body*. Ill. B. Degen. New York: Scholastic.

Conrad, P. (1995). *Call me Ahnighito*. Ill. R. Egielski. New York: HarperCollins.

Cullen, E. (1996). *Spiders*. New York: Mondo. (Original work published 1986)

dePaola, T. (1973). *Charlie needs a cloak*. New York: Simon & Schuster.

dePaola, T. (1978). *The popcorn book*. New York: Holiday House.

Earle, A. (1995). *Zipping, zapping, zooming bats*. Ill. H. Cole. New York: HarperCollins.

Ehlert, L. (1987). *Growing vegetable soup*. New York: Scholastic.

Farndon, J., & Kirkwood, J. (1998). *The Kingfisher first animal encyclopedia*. New York: Kingfisher.

Feely, J. (1999). *Shadow puppets*. Ill. A. Stitt. Photo. R. Tonkin. Littleton, MA: Sundance.

Fowler, A. (1996). *Life in a pond*. New York: Children's Book Press.

George, J.C. (1995). *Everglades*. Ill. W. Minor. New York: HarperCollins.

Gibbons, G. (1989). *Monarch butterfly*. New York: Scholastic.

Gibbons, G. (1995). *The reasons for seasons*. New York: Holiday House.

Gibbons, G. (2001). *Ducks!* New York: Holiday House.

Gibbons, G. (2001). *Polar bears*. New York: Holiday House.

Graham, J.B. (1994). *Splish splash*. Boston: Houghton Mifflin.
Heller, R. (1983). *The reason for a flower*. New York: Scholastic.
High, L.O. (2001). *Under New York*. Ill. R. Rayevsky. New York: Holiday House.
Hoffman, M. (1986). *Snake*. Milwaukee, WI: Raintree.
Isaacs, S.S. (2000). *Life in America's first cities*. Chicago: Heinemann Library.
Isaacs, S.S. (2002). *Life on the underground railroad*. Chicago: Heinemann Library.
James, S. (1991). *Dear Mr. Blueberry*. New York: Maxwell Macmillan International.
James, S.M. (2002). *Dolphins*. New York. Mondo.
James, S.M. (2002). *Seahorses*. New York: Mondo.
Jenkins, M. (1999). *The emperor's egg*. Ill. J. Chapman. Cambridge, MA: Candlewick Press.
Jenkins, S. (1995). *Biggest, strongest, fastest*. New York: Scholastic.
Jenkins, S. (2001). *Slap, squeak & scatter: How animals communicate*. Boston: Houghton Mifflin.
Kalman, B., & Everts, T. (1994). *Bears*. New York: Crabtree.
Kerrod, R. (1992). *Amazing flying machines*. Ill. M. Dunning. New York: Knopf.
King-Smith, D. (1994). *I love guinea pigs*. Ill. A. Jeram. Cambridge, MA: Candlewick Press.
Kramer, S. (1992). *Lightning*. Photo. W. Faidley. Minneapolis, MN: Carolrhoda.
Kroll, S. (1994). *Lewis and Clark: Explorers of the American West*. Ill. R. Williams. New York: Holiday House.
Lassieur, A. (2002). *The Hopi*. Mankato, MN: Bridgestone Books.
Lessor, B. (2004). *Trees*. Ill. A. Salesse. New York: Mondo.
Lobel, A. (1979). *Frog and toad are friends*. New York: HarperCollins.
Lollis, S. (with J. Hogan and her second-grade class). (2003). *Should we have pets? A persuasive text*. New York: Mondo.
Looye, J.U. (1998). *Body numbers*. Barrington, IL: Ribgy.
Lucero, J. (1996). *How to make salsa*. Ill. F.X. Mora. New York: Mondo.
Macaulay, D. (1973). *Cathedral: The Story of Its Construction*. Boston: Houghton Mifflin.
Machotka, H. (1991). *What neat feet!* New York: William Morrow.
Markle, S. (2001). *Growing up wild: Wolves*. New York: Simon & Schuster.
Martin, J.B. (1998). *Snowflake Bentley*. Ill. M. Azarian. Boston: Houghton Mifflin.
Martin-James, K. (2001). *Soaring bald eagles*. Minneapolis, MN: Lerner.
Marzollo, J. (1988). *I am a leaf*. Ill. J. Moffat. New York: Scholastic.
Meadows, G., & Vail, C. (2000). *Lions*. Carlsbad, CA: Dominie Press.
Meadows, G., & Vail, C. (2002). *Cheetahs*. Carlsbad, CA: Dominie Press.
Meadows, G., & Vail, C. (2002). *Reptiles*. Carlsbad, CA: Dominie Press.
Meadows, G., & Vail, C. (2003). *Wasps & bees*. Carlsbad, CA: Dominie Press.
Meadows, G., & Vail, C. *Arctic foxes and red foxes*. Carlsbad, CA: Dominie Press.

Merrick, P. (2000). *Bears*. Chanhassen, MN: The Child's World.

Micucci, C. (1997). *The life and times of the peanut*. Boston: Houghton Mifflin.

Miller, M. (1998). *Cats*. Des Plaines, IL: Heinemann Library.

Miller, M. (1998). *Dogs*. Des Plaines, IL: Heinemann Library.

Minarik, E.H. (2003). *Little Bear*. Ill. M. Sendak. New York: HarperTrophy.

Morris, N. (1996). *Deserts*. New York: Crabtree.

Murray, S. (2001). *Wild West*. New York: Dorling Kindersley.

Nelson, R. (2003). *From wax to crayon*. Minneapolis, MN: Lerner.

O'Brien, P. (1999). *How big were the dinosaurs? Gigantic!* New York: Henry Holt.

Parsons, A. (1990). *Amazing snakes*. Photo. J. Young. New York: Knopf.

Patten, J.M. (1995). *Solids, liquids and gases*. Vero Beach, FL: Rourke.

Perez, M. (2000). *Breakfast around the world*. Bothell, WA: The Wright Group.

Pinkney, A.D. (1998). *Duke Ellington*. Ill. B. Pinkney. New York: Hyperion.

Relf, P. (1996). *The Magic School Bus wet all over: A book about the water cycle*. New York: Scholastic.

Relf, P. (2000). *What's happening? A book of explanations*. Ill. F.H. Schwartz. New York: Mondo.

Robinson, C. (1997). *Penguins*. Crystal Lake, IL: Heinemann Library.

Rockwell, A., (2001). *Bugs are insects*. Ill. S. Jenkins. New York: HarperCollins.

Royston, A. (1991).*Jungle animals*. Photo. P. Dowell. New York: Simon & Schuster.

Roza, G. (2003). *A primary source guide to China*. New York: Rosen.

Saunders-Smith, G. (1998). *Leaves*. Mankato, MN: Capstone Press.

Schwartz, D.M. (1999). *If you hopped like a frog*. Ill. J. Warhola. New York: Scholastic.

Seuss, Dr. (1968). *The foot book*. New York: Random House.

Short, J., Green, J., & Bird, B. (1997). *Platypus*. Ill. A. Wichlinski. New York: Mondo.

Sill, C. (1997). *About mammals: A guide for children*. Ill. J. Sill. Atlanta, GA: Peachtree.

Simon, S. (1988). *Galaxies*. New York: Morrow.

Simon, S. (1994). *Comets, meteors, and asteroids*. New York: William Morrow.

Smith, C. (1996). *How to draw trucks and cars*. Milwaukee, WI: Gareth Stevens.

Snowball, D. (1994). *Exploring freshwater habitats*. Ill. C. Belcher & M. Katin. New York: Mondo.

Stanley, D., & Vennema, P. (1992). *Bard of Avon: The story of William Shakespeare*. Ill. D. Stanley. New York: Morrow.

Taberski, S. (and her first-grade class). (2002). *Penguins are waterbirds*. New York: Mondo.

Taylor, B., & Holland, S. (2002). *Reptiles*. New York: Dorling Kindersley.

Theodorou, R. (1998). *Animal legs*. Barrington, IL: Rigby.

Theodorou, R. (1998). *Prehistoric record breakers*. Crystal Lake, IL: Rigby.

Theodorou, R. (2000). *Mammals*. Chicago: Heinemann Library.

Walker, S., & Gray, S. (2001). *Dinosaur*. New York: Dorling Kindersley.

Wallace, K. (2000). *Big machines*. New York: Dorling Kindersley.

Wallner, A. (1994). *Betsy Ross*. New York: Holiday House.

Warshaw, H. (2000). *The sleepover cookbook*. Photo. J. Brown. New York: Sterling.

Wilkes, A. (1990). *Deserts*. Ill. P. Dennis. London: Usborne.

Zoehfeld, K.W. (2001). *Terrible tryannosaurs*. Ill. L. Washburn. New York: HarperCollins.

Note: Page numbers followed by *f* indicate figures and by *t* indicate tables.

H

I

J

K

Q

R

T–U

V